'This book argues that sustaining humane welfare states is a matter of political will. Modern welfare states face many challenges from neo-liberalism, austerity, globalization, population ageing and the emergence of new social risks. None of these challenges is insuperable. The real question is whether the political solidarities on which the welfare state was founded can be renewed in a more open and unequal world.'

Peter Taylor-Gooby, University of Kent

'At moments of great economic uncertainty and social insecurity, it is wise to count one's blessings. In this marvellously concise and timely essay Andrew Gamble, one of Britain's most prolific political commentators, steers clear of nostalgia. There is no ground for retrospective 'ill fares the land' melancholia. Capitalism, democracy and modern welfare provision can only prosper in sync. The welfare state is an integrative institution – not a divisive one. But this general lesson requires a strong reformist political commitment to invest in a future-oriented social infrastructure for rich twenty-first century capitalist democracies. This political commitment cannot be taken for granted at a time when many citizens and politicians wrongly believe that the welfare state era is over. Sobering but extremely important reading for all who care.'

Anton Hemerijck, VU University Amsterdam and the London School of Economics and Political Science

Can the Welfare State Survive?

Global Futures Series

Andrew Gamble

———

Can the Welfare State Survive?

polity

First published in 2016 by Polity Press

Polity Press
65 Bridge Street
Cambridge CB2 1UR, UK

Polity Press
350 Main Street
Malden, MA 02148, USA

ISBN-13: 978-0-7456-9873-1
ISBN-13: 978-0-7456-9874-8(pb)

Library of Congress Cataloging-in-Publication Data
Names: Gamble, Andrew, author.
Title: Can the welfare state survive? / Andrew Gamble.
Description: Malden, MA ¬†: Polity, 2016. | Includes bibliographical
   references.
Identifiers: LCCN 2015035196| ISBN 9780745698731 (hardback) | ISBN
   9780745698748 (paperback)
Subjects: LCSH: Welfare state. | BISAC: POLITICAL SCIENCE / General.
Classification: LCC JC479 .G36 2016 | DDC 361.6/5--dc23 LC record available at
http://lccn.loc.gov/2015035196

Typeset in 11 on 15 pt Sabon by
Servis Filmsetting Ltd, Stockport, Cheshire
Printed and bound in Great Britain by CPI Group (UK) Ltd, Croydon

For further information on Polity, visit our website:
politybooks.com

Contents

In memory of my mother and father,
Joan Westall, 1919–2015
Marc Gamble, 1914–2007

Introduction

Can the welfare state survive? Yes, I think it can. It might seem strange even to pose the question. Western societies have grown steadily richer and safer over the seventy years since the Second World War. The establishment and extension of welfare states over this period has been one of the proudest achievements and most obvious fruits of Western prosperity. It is one of the features which makes rich societies distinctive. Pooling collective risks over the life-cycle, redistributing between the generations to provide a better, more secure existence for everybody, alleviating poverty – who can be seriously opposed to that? Yet all is not well with our welfare states. The richer we become, the less willing and able we seem to be to pay for them. We hear constantly of underfunding, of a looming crisis of entitlements, of costs escalating and service standards slipping. For many decades now, welfare states of all kinds have been under siege, even in times of prosperity and economic growth. Their era of expansion came to an end in the 1970s, and since then they have entered an era of permanent austerity. There have been constant complaints that welfare states are becoming unaffordable, are wasteful and inefficient, and are in need of drastic reform. During the 1990s, far-reaching reforms were launched which seemed for a time to offer them a new political foundation. But since the financial crash in 2008 and its troubled aftermath, they have had to confront a new era of retrenchment and austerity. New struggles have erupted over which welfare programmes should be protected and which should be axed or scaled back, and there are those who dare to think the unthinkable and wonder whether we need a welfare *state* at all. Is the welfare state out of time, a relic of the industrial capitalist past, which may once have had its place, but increasingly jars with the political economy of the twenty-first century and should be dismantled?

What do we mean by welfare? The *Oxford English Dictionary* defines it as the state or condition of doing or being well; good fortune, happiness or well-being; prosperity. 'Well fare you' in the sixteenth century meant 'May it go well with you.'

Everyone wants to fare well, to have opportunities, good health and education, to enjoy protection against the risks of being unable to earn a living through ill health, injury, or unemployment, and to have access to the basic resources needed to live a full life. But why do we need the state to be involved? This is where the controversy lies. The role of states in providing welfare has taken different forms, which explains why the American definition of 'welfare' is very different from the European one. In the United States, welfare is defined narrowly to mean income transfers or direct services which support the poor and give them a minimum standard of living. For Europeans, welfare is defined broadly to include not just redistribution to the poor, but also spending to pool collective risks and to provide investment in the human capital of all citizens. It therefore includes spending on health, education, and pensions. If the welfare state is understood only to concern the poor, the majority of citizens will have no stake in it, but they will have a very big stake if it includes the mainstream services which all citizens use at different stages of their lives.[1]

In exploring whether the welfare state can survive, I will use the broad rather than the narrow definition of welfare. Welfare states as they have evolved have come to be concerned with much more than just providing a safety net. Pinning down what is meant by a welfare state is important because it affects the definition of 'survival'. If measured purely by spending, the welfare state appears to be in rude health, even in the midst of austerity and cuts. But these aggregate figures often do not reflect qualitative changes in the way welfare states operate. Welfare spending may be as high as ever, but what comfort is that if welfare states no longer protect citizens against risks in the way they once did, or if they are becoming much more punitive to the poor? In an era of retrenchment, welfare states are put under extreme pressure. This raises the interesting question: at what point does the welfare state cease to be a welfare state? This question is part normative and part empirical. The normative part is whether the welfare state should survive, meaning whether it deserves to survive, which is separate from the empirical question of whether it will survive. You can argue, as many market libertarians do, that the welfare state should not survive, while concluding gloomily that it very probably will, because the political obstacles to dismantling it are too great. Among supporters of the welfare state, there are those like Paul Pierson, who fears it is unlikely to survive for much longer because the very features which made it so resilient in the past have also made it virtually incapable of reform, and now very vulnerable in the new circumstances that have emerged in the aftermath of the financial crisis.[2] A contrasting view is held by those like Anton Hemerijck, who, while acknowledging the peril facing welfare states, argues that the crisis creates the opportunity for reform and a new advance for the welfare state.[3] I agree with Hemerijck. The welfare state can survive, but only if some of the key challenges which it faces are addressed through a new politics. Its survival is not guaranteed or certain, but it is possible.

There are four key challenges which the welfare state faces. The first is *affordability* – the perpetual task of reconciling resources with expectations. How can the welfare state survive if it is starved of the resources it requires because its citizens will the end but not the means? They want high-quality public services but are reluctant to pay the taxes to fund them. As the welfare state has expanded, so the expectations of citizens have risen, fuelled by competition between political parties to secure votes. In the initial phase of the development of the welfare state, the cost was easier to carry. But as the programmes have matured, the long-term funding implications of many of the programmes, like pensions, have loomed larger. Projected forward, these costs rise exponentially, suggesting severe fiscal squeezes to come unless programmes are made much less generous or citizens agree to higher taxes.

The second challenge is *international competitiveness*. How can the welfare state survive when many of the new rising powers in the world are developing forms of capitalism which are not burdened by welfare costs? The higher costs of labour in the rich economies make them uncompetitive with labour elsewhere. Many fear that the rents in the form of higher incomes and profits which the Western world has extracted for several centuries are gradually being eroded and with them the fiscal base for the welfare state, and the social contract which has sustained it. This is not a new problem. The same fears were raised in the past about globalization and the 'race to the bottom'. These fears proved unfounded, because many welfare states proved resilient.[4] But with the arrival of new hard times since the financial crash, these fears have surfaced once again.

The third challenge is *new social risks*. Can the welfare state be adapted to cope with the very different economic and social landscape of contemporary advanced capitalist societies? The welfare state developed in an era of big government, big companies, and big unions. It shared the collective ethic and purpose of many of these institutions. It was a natural counterpart to the modern industrial societies which were pioneered in the United States and Germany in the first half of the twentieth century. With the decline of mass manufacturing and the rise of service economies, contemporary market societies have placed ever greater emphasis on individual initiative and responsibility, eroding many of the collective structures and organizations, like trade unions, which supported collective action in the past and created political support for the welfare state. New social risks arise from the changing role of women in the workforce, the weakening of the traditional form of the household, the importance of social care, and new vulnerabilities of individuals in a rapidly changing labour market because of their low or inadequate skills and the insecurity of so many jobs.

The fourth challenge is *ageing*. Can the welfare state adjust to the demographic shift to an ageing population? Many mature welfare states face a challenge from an increase in the ratio of older citizens to younger citizens. Old people are living longer and fertility rates are declining. In part this is due to the success of the welfare state in promoting better and more universal health care, investing in public health, and making it possible for many more women to enter the workforce. People are living beyond the ages assumed in the early years of welfare states. At the same time, rates of population growth are decreasing in many countries, and immigration, which might offer a remedy, is being discouraged. The consequence is a steadily increasing cost of supporting the elderly, much of which falls on the younger generation.

These four challenges pose a number of intractable dilemmas for governments, since they cannot be wished away, and managing them requires confronting a number of unwelcome choices. As in many areas of modern government, this leads to decisions being endlessly postponed, in the hope that something will turn up, or that the problem will miraculously solve itself. Critics of the welfare state argue that these dilemmas are insoluble and that they undermine the case for continuing with a welfare state at all. The failures of the welfare state cannot be fixed, and whether people want it to survive or not, it is becoming increasingly dysfunctional and cannot be sustained indefinitely. Much of the extended state built up over the last hundred years should be dismantled, and we should return to an era of small states which spend no more than 15–20 per cent of national income (as compared with 40–50 per cent today).

Introduction

If the welfare state is to survive, its supporters have not just to explain why it deserves to survive but also to analyse the challenges which threaten to undermine its effectiveness and its legitimacy and suggest ways they might be overcome. This is what this book attempts to do. I explore the arguments for and against the welfare state, outline how we got to where we are, explore some of the debates around the welfare state, and discuss challenges and future trajectories. I argue that despite its many shortcomings, the welfare state is not about to disappear and can be reformed in ways which strengthen its prospects for long-term survival. But it will need political imagination and political will, and a willingness to confront obstacles to change.

The reason to be optimistic about the future of the welfare state is that the basic political and economic reasons why it first emerged have not gone away. There is a great deal of evidence suggesting that welfare states are resilient, even when the political and economic climate is very hostile. Yet it would be foolish to deny that the challenges welfare states face are deep and perplexing. It is perfectly possible to imagine how a political momentum could develop in particular Western countries, particularly in some of the states within Anglo-America, which could lead to the gradual

dismantling of the welfare state and the entrench-
ment of a much more unequal and stratified form
of capitalism. There is nothing inevitable about
this. It is a matter of political choice and political
decision. There are powerful constraints preventing
the extension of the welfare state, but there are also
powerful constraints preventing its dismantling.
Despite the crash, neo-liberal ideas are still dominant and alternatives are lacking. There is currently
a deadlock.[5] How it is resolved politically in different countries will determine what kind of welfare
state will survive, and indeed whether the welfare
state will survive at all.

1

The Life and Times of the Welfare State

For more than one hundred years the welfare state has been an integral part of the most successful and advanced capitalist economies. It has commanded support from all parts of the political spectrum, and although in the twentieth century it became particularly identified with parties of the labour movement and the democratic Left, it was at first principally associated with politicians of the Right and Centre-Right, including Conservative aristocrats like Otto von Bismarck in Germany and Liberal industrialists like Joseph Chamberlain in England. Many representatives of the propertied classes in the nineteenth century backed the development of state-funded welfare programmes to provide greater security to the urban working class and shield them from some of the uncertainties of the market, principally through the provision of unemployment pay and pensions. Most working people had no property or assets, and were therefore always at risk of being plunged into dire poverty by losing their job, falling ill, growing old, or losing the main breadwinner in the family through death or desertion. Misfortunes could strike without warning, creating great uncertainty even during good times.

There was a steadily growing acceptance that something needed to be done for the working poor, particularly the deserving poor, those who worked hard and did the right thing, but suffered hardship and misfortune through no fault of their own. The Christian Churches played an important role in changing opinion. But if compassion played a role, fear was also a powerful motivation. Bismarck was concerned to stop the rise of the socialist movement in Germany by seeking to divide it and make workers dependent on the German state for their welfare. Chamberlain declared bluntly that property must pay a ransom if it wanted to keep its privileges. This view was widely shared across Europe. The dazzling display of Edwardian England and *La Belle Époque* in France reflected both the vast wealth which nineteenth-century capitalism had created and its very unequal distribution. Wealth was more concentrated than it has been at any time since, and the sharp contrast between the wealth of the propertied and the poverty and insecurity of the great majority of working people helped fuel radical anti-capitalist movements of the Left.

Providing welfare through the state was conceived as a means of protecting property and deflecting popular protest by giving the poor a greater stake in the political system, proving that the state could act for them and not only for the wealthy. Helping the poor in this way was deeply controversial, but it was justified both on grounds of paternalism – the poor deserved the help of the community – and on grounds of expediency – guaranteeing a minimum level of income and security, countering catastrophic declines in income for households, was a small cost if it helped avert social disorder and social revolution. Critics warned, as they have been warning ever since, that it was a slippery slope. Once the state took responsibility for providing economic security to the poor, it would remove the incentives to work and create an ever-growing number of dependants. Herbert Spencer spoke for many Liberals across Europe. If someone ended up in the gutter, it was their own fault, and the state should not step in to protect them from the conse-quences of their folly.

This view was widely held, but it did not ulti-mately prevail. The gaps in private and voluntary provision of welfare were too large, and using the fiscal and organizational power of the state to remedy them had many advantages. Coverage could be made comprehensive, and a set of common rules applied to all. Most of the early schemes were not particularly generous and were closely tied to an insurance principle. Workers paid in to the scheme and then were guaranteed payouts when they needed them. In this way, individual responsibility and self-reliance were preserved. And there was minimal interference with the market order. What the state ensured was that the funds would always be there when they were required, which helped reduce insecurity.

The first welfare states therefore emerged as a moral response to the plight of the working poor in the new industrial capitalism, as well as a pragmatic response to the political danger of the state turning its back on the working class, which was beginning to organize in its own self-defence. But there were also other powerful reasons for the rise of welfare states, apart from morality and expediency. Modern industrial economies needed healthier, better-educated, and better-paid workers if they were to reach their full potential. Markets were seen as too slow, too uncertain, too wasteful, too selective, to provide what was needed, and the gaps could only be partly filled by families. Expanding the state became the solution. The new collectivism on both right and left regarded the modern state as an enterprise, a command economy, a military operation, which could cut through the waste and inefficiency of laissez-faire capitalism and mobilize the full potential of each nation.

Welfare states were also about nation-building, the creation of a common citizenship. Modern citizens were all members of the same nation and as such had certain entitlements and expectations as well as obligations and responsibilities. Each nation was a community of fate. Citizens depended upon one another; their fate was inextricably bound up with that of all other citizens in the national community. This meant that the state, too, had both an obligation to maximize the potential of every citizen and an interest in doing so. Providing the best possible education, the best health care, the best opportunities for creativity and training – all these became both what modern citizens expected and modern governments strove to deliver. Nations were competing with other nations, so governments could not afford to neglect their most valuable resource, their own people.

The new nationalism in Europe and the pressure for the state to extend its role and its capacities were closely linked to the spread of democracy. At the end of the nineteenth century, political power in Europe was still in the hands of a narrow political class, its position protected by a restricted franchise. The labour movements of European social democracy were anti-state movements because the state was the monopoly of the propertied classes, both aristocratic and capitalist. Many of these movements established their own institutions outside the state to pool risk and protect their members. There were important strands of cooperative and labour movements which were both anti-capitalist and anti-state. They sought to create a protected sphere outside both the existing state and the market to provide for needs which the state would not recognize and to protect against the uncertainties and risks of a market economy. This was a form of collective self-reliance, to mitigate some of the effects of the capitalist market, but the power of those institutions was limited.

All this was to change as the vote was extended to all citizens, both men and women, across Europe following the end of the First World War. Parties of the democratic Left developed a new strategy to achieve their aims, which involved gaining political power through the institutions of representative democracy, by winning parliamentary majorities and taking control of the existing apparatus of the state bureaucracy to implement their programmes. After some intense struggles, agreement gradually emerged across the political spectrum not only that welfare programmes were desirable, but also that they should be either provided through the state or underpinned by it. Parties of the Centre-Right, influenced by Catholic social teaching, also emerged as champions of particular kinds of welfare state. The argument between parties of right and left was increasingly over how generous state welfare provision should be, and how much redistribution should be involved, not over the principle itself. Progress was still slow, however, in part because the fiscal base of the nineteenth-century tax state was geared to the interests of the propertied class and was far too narrow to provide the kind of funds necessary to support universal welfare programmes. But during the first half of the twentieth century, collectivist remedies and approaches were gradually adopted, and ways were found to enlarge the capacity of the state to impose and collect taxes. War was a great catalyst in this respect. The need to enlarge the state to secure national survival in an era of total war obliged governments to find new sources of revenue for weapons and armies. They simultaneously acquired new powers to control and plan many different aspects of modern society. Once the state had expanded, it was hard to shrink it back to its former size. The old liberal political economy, with its doctrines of individualism and laissez-faire and its suspicion of the state and the centralization and concentration of power, fell under a cloud for a time, even in its Anglo-American heartlands.

One of the reasons for this was the spectacular crash on Wall Street in 1929, which was followed by the fragmentation of the international economic order, the collapse of the gold standard, economic stagnation and depression in many countries, and the emergence of economic and military blocs. These events strengthened the argument that the reforms already achieved had not gone far enough. Capitalism had to be fundamentally reorganized to provide a basic minimum of income and security for every citizen. How this was to be done was at first unclear. Piecemeal incremental reform was the pattern in the 1930s. What transformed the situation and provided the opportunity for a much more general reconstruction of the domestic and international political economy was the outbreak once again of world war, this time on a new and terrifying scale. The intensity of the struggle for national survival brought with it the demand for a new domestic order as well as a new world order. If nations could organize themselves so effectively for war, they could also deliver a lasting and prosperous peace, based on welfare and security for all.

The new mood and purpose found expression in the Beveridge Report, published in the United Kingdom in December 1942, which characterized the problem facing Western societies in terms of the five giants of Want, Idleness, Disease, Ignorance, and Squalor.[1] The remedies proposed and adopted in more and more countries after 1945 were universal programmes of social security, health, education, and housing, funded through much higher levels of taxation. The insurance principle still lay at the heart of these welfare states. Redistribution was primarily between different generations and between people at different stages of their lives. But there was also much greater taxation of property, both income and wealth, as a result of the war and its dislocations, and so after the war the propertied classes throughout the Western economies were generally paying more towards state programmes than they had ever done in the past, and more than they were ever to do again.

All the European economies had a painful period of reconstruction after 1945, to overcome the huge destruction of physical and human capital during the war. But once this period of often dire poverty and hardship had been navigated, the Western economies, far from lapsing back into stagnation and slow growth, as many had feared, instead embarked on the most successful period of growth and prosperity in the history of capitalism. The new expanded welfare states played their part in this, although they were not the only cause. Defence and rearmament and the expansion of new technologies were also important. The economic success meant that welfare states were accepted as never before as a crucial component of a legitimate market order. Competition with the Soviet Union played a part too. Western states were determined to resist internal subversion and to show that their model of political economy was superior. Generous welfare states and high and rising living standards were crucial components of the Western model. Over time this model outperformed its rival. But it did more than that. The remarkable success of Western capitalist economies in the 1950s and 1960s led many to assume that the secret of stable and prosperous democratic capitalism had been discovered. There was a class compromise and social peace unimaginable to those who had experienced the deeply divided class societies of the past. The essence of the compromise was described by Seymour Martin Lipset.[2] Conservatives accepted that there should be a generous welfare state for all citizens, while socialists accepted that not all economic power should be concentrated in the hands of the state.

This period in which the welfare state was relatively uncontested was short-lived. It was a time of falling inequality, rising social mobility, and high levels of political participation, as well as high employment, low inflation, and rapid rises in productivity, output, and wages. For many on the democratic Left, the period appeared to show that democracy and capitalism could co-exist, and that if social democracy was strong and vigilant enough, capitalism could be tamed, and its energies channelled in ways which aided rather than undermined social cohesion. The expanded welfare programmes paid for by high and progressive taxes were one of the main signs of this. The Right, too, accepted the new dispensation as a reasonable compromise. Many of the welfare regimes which emerged across Europe were shaped by the parties of Christian Democracy. There were some who were not reconciled to the compromise, fearing the long-term erosion of liberty, and worrying with Friedrich Hayek that Western societies had embarked on a road to serfdom.[3] But more agreed with Karl Polanyi that nineteenth-century capitalism had been unsustainable. It was so destructive of the

21

conditions for stable societies that it had provoked a strong reaction from both right and left, and the imposing of new rules and restrictions on how capitalism operated so as to protect the interests of the majority.[4] What was surprising to many observers was that a much larger state, greatly expanded welfare provision, and the strengthening of the position of organized labour proved compatible with an expanding and reinvigorated private sector.

What undermined this settlement was the end of the boom and the emergence of a new set of economic problems which produced higher inflation and low growth, the stagflation of the 1970s. The United States was no longer willing to sustain the international monetary order under the same conditions as had existed since the 1940s and set about restructuring it. Domestic political conflict intensified and opinion polarized over how best to deal with rising inflation and the trade union militancy which was one of its effects. The impact of this crisis was uneven, but in those countries hit hardest, one of the central issues of dispute came to be the welfare state. Had it grown too big, and become too expensive? Was it now too much of a burden on the wealth-producing sectors of the economy, inhibiting rather than facilitating growth? One influential text produced at this time by two

Oxford economists, Roger Bacon and Walter Eltis, argued that most of the public sector, including the welfare state, did not produce any wealth in itself, but instead was parasitical upon the private sector. The solution to the problems of the British economy in the 1970s, and by extension those of all the advanced economies, was to cut back sharply on both employment and output in the public sector to make room for private investment and private profits.[5] This argument was a new statement of the old Treasury view from the 1920s and 1930s which had so vexed John Maynard Keynes. It stated simply that any expansion in public spending would always be at the expense of private spending and investment.[6] Since the latter was assumed to be more economically efficient, the effect would be to impoverish the economy. The modern jargon is 'crowding out'. Public sector spending and investment crowd out investment and spending by the private sector. It followed that in a period of slow growth and inflationary pressure, the correct policy response is to scale back public spending, including welfare spending.

The political struggle over taxes and spending in the 1970s changed the terms of the debate about the welfare state in the liberal political economies of Anglo-America, and marked the beginning of a major divergence between these welfare regimes and those elsewhere in Europe. In Anglo-America, the welfare state came to be seen as no longer a condition for growth and prosperity but a potential barrier and obstacle to it. Welfare spending was only affordable when the economy was growing strongly and should be cut back if the economy stalled. Following the upheavals of the 1970s, a new set of policy priorities came to be established in both the United States and the United Kingdom in the following decade. In the much more open world economy which ensued after the dismantling of the Bretton Woods fixed exchange rate regime, national economies had much less protection from the international financial markets, and a series of neo-liberal reforms were introduced in many countries: the ending of capital controls, deregulation and privatization, lowering of taxes on income and wealth, and the weakening of employment rights and trade unions to create flexible labour markets.

Even in those states which went furthest in experimenting with neo-liberal arrangements, the welfare state did not disappear. Indeed, in important respects it continued to expand, although in different ways and to a different extent depending on local political circumstances. In some countries, there were political attempts to dismantle parts of the welfare state, and there was strong pressure to contain it and shrink it. In other countries, the pressure to cut back welfare was much less marked, and some even continued to expand their welfare provision. There had always been differences among the Western economies in the size and scope of their welfare states, reflecting the different political coalitions which had created and sustained them, but in the 1980s and 1990s this became more marked. This divergence in the character of welfare states was termed by Gøsta Esping-Andersen 'the three worlds of welfare capitalism'. He distinguished between the generous Nordic social democratic welfare states in Scandinavia, the hierarchical corporatist welfare states found particularly in the German-speaking world, and the residual liberal welfare states found in the states of Anglo-America.[7] The divergence between these three models had become significant, although Esping-Andersen noted that even the residual welfare states were still recognizably welfare states in providing collective programmes to combat insecurity arising from the life-cycle or the labour market, and there were still important universal programmes, like the British National Health Service, which remained free at the point of use. All three models delivered welfare through a combination of markets, households, and states, but differed in the relative emphasis they placed on each. Liberal welfare states relied more heavily on markets, conservative welfare state on households, especially traditional forms of the family, and social democratic welfare states on the state.

Esping-Andersen's work was important also for the new clarity he brought to defining the welfare state. He criticized models which defined this by how much governments spent on welfare, arguing that welfare state regimes needed to be grasped as coherent wholes, created through the interaction of states, markets, and households, and reflecting particular class coalitions of interests, which led to different rules, institutions and policies, and outcomes. For Esping-Andersen, the most important way of differentiating welfare state programmes and welfare state regimes was whether they allowed individuals to escape from dependence on the market or whether they confirmed that dependence. The promise of the welfare state as it has unfolded is that all citizens gain social rights which are inviolable, granted on the basis of citizenship rather than performance in the market. This means that citizens are no longer forced to meet all their needs and those of their dependants through the market wage they can command, or to deal individually with all the uncertainties of unemployment, sickness, injury, and old age. Instead, their basic human needs for security are met by the collective provision of services and support outside the market. 'Decommodification' of labour means that workers are freed from market disciplines through the collective pooling of risks and the recognition of their social rights. Esping-Andersen identifies the trend to decommodify labour as the fundamental logic of the welfare state, and what makes it not subordinate but complementary to the market.

Welfare state regimes diverged more sharply in the neo-liberal era than they did before it, but even in those countries where the reaction against 'welfarism' was strongest, the United States and the United Kingdom, there was still strong political resistance to welfare cuts. Radical right governments like the Reagan administration in the United States and the Thatcher government in the United Kingdom made much less progress in 'rolling back the state' than their rhetoric suggested.[8] Electoral politics was one constraint – many of the universal programmes were popular and governments were wary of meddling with them. There were also powerful vested interests which defended existing levels of provision, not least the large numbers of private companies which were dependent on public contracts to supply services and equipment for the main welfare programmes. Retrenchment proved to have definite political limits.

Neo-liberalism was not a single doctrine. There were several significant strands, including a laissez-faire strand, which emphasized market freedom, a social investment strand, which emphasized investment in human capital, and an ordo-liberal strand, which emphasized fiscal balance and rule-based policy-making. The international framework within which all governments had to work was neo-liberal, reflecting the reshaping of the rules governing the international market order in the 1970s and 1980s. But within this framework there were many different possibilities, and there was certainly no uniformity or pressure to converge. Some governments experimented with Third Way policies of social investment combining economic efficiency and social justice.[9] They accepted many of the domestic neo-liberal reforms undertaken in the 1980s, but were still able to increase significantly the proportion of national income spent collectively on welfare. Critics of the Third Way argued that it continued the erosion of the non-market sphere and made welfare states dependent once again on markets and market criteria. But it also demonstrated that it was perfectly possible even within the liberal market economies of Anglo-America to give a high priority to the welfare state, and to find ways to expand it again, in terms of both spending and employment.

The 1970s was a period of crisis for the welfare state, the first time the momentum of its development had been slowed, and the first time since its inception that serious questions had been raised as to whether its continued expansion was still desirable. There were numerous radical right and market libertarian analyses of why the welfare state was so flawed. At the other end of the political spectrum, many on the Marxist Left also became strong critics of welfare developed through the state. But as Claus Offe argued, the problem for capitalism was that it could no longer live with the welfare state, but it could also no longer live without it.[10] This has remained the problem up to the present. Many of the more ambitious attempts to dismantle the post-war welfare states had only limited success in the neo-liberal era, and the staying power of the welfare state and even its 'irreversibility' seemed to be confirmed by empirical studies. It had become embedded in both the politics and the political economy of all the Western economies. There were many different welfare state regimes, and researchers added several more to the three core clusters identified by Esping-Andersen, but all recognizably belonged to the process which had so transformed the laissez-faire capitalism of the nineteenth century and laid the foundations of the organized capitalism of the twentieth. Welfare capitalism had become the norm for all the advanced capitalist economies. The scope and scale of the state had been transformed to help sustain and reproduce the capitalist order.

This conclusion seemed confirmed by the impetus which developed in the 1990s and early 2000s to reform existing welfare states rather than merely retrench them, adapting them to take account of the rise of new social risks and changes in employment patterns and in the composition of households. The social investment welfare state was most evident in the social democratic welfare regimes of the Nordic countries, but it also strongly influenced the Neue Mitte in Germany and the Third Way in the United Kingdom. The emphasis was placed on the need for the welfare state to be active rather than passive, and to engage in continuous reform in order to ensure that it remained both affordable and capable of delivering the kind of services and the quality of services which citizens demanded.

In the twenty-first century, however, the future of the welfare state has again been questioned. The neo-liberal order, like the Keynesian order before it, developed its own pathologies which combined to deliver the financial crash in 2008. The meltdown of the financial system was narrowly averted, but at the cost of a severe recession in 2009, followed by a long-drawn-out recovery, the slowest since 1945. Even in 2015, some countries had not regained their pre-crash level of output, interest rates remained at rock bottom, quantitative easing had been employed on a massive scale by central banks to improve banks' balance sheets and keep asset prices high, and growth and productivity remained subdued in most economies and the prospects uncertain.[11] Against this background, a new political conflict over distribution and growth developed, both within national political economies and between them, as, for example, in the case of the eurozone. A politics of austerity became established, especially in Europe, which advocated fiscal consolidation as the correct policy response to the financial crisis and the recession, cutting back public spending, and welfare spending in particular, in order to eliminate budget deficits and bring down spiralling national debts.[12]

This crisis, for which there is as yet no end in sight, has posed a great challenge once more to the welfare state. If the neo-liberal growth model cannot be restored, the Western economies may be condemned to a long period of secular stagnation:

slow growth, stagnant living standards for the majority, rising inequality, and persistent pressure towards deflation. Such a situation would be extremely testing for the survival of welfare states, and already there has been a revival of calls for radical surgery to existing welfare states, dismantling much of the structure of collective welfare provision built up over the last century. Radical right ideas have made big inroads into the Republican Party in the United States. Rand Paul, one of the contenders for the Republican presidential nomination in 2016, and Paul Ryan, who was the Republican nominee for Vice President in 2012, have put forward ambitious plans for returning the size of the federal state to nineteenth-century levels. The current crisis has revived many of the critiques of the welfare state which were first formed in the 1970s. The buoyancy of the international economy in the 1990s and early 2000s, in part supported by the strong performance of the rising powers, China, India, and Brazil, had blunted the edge of these critiques. But the financial crash has revived them. The questions are posed once again with special urgency whether the welfare state should and will survive, and whether it retains the moral legitimacy or practical capacity to do so.

2

The Battle of Ideas

The creation, maintenance, and future of the welfare state has never been just a question of political economy narrowly conceived. It has also always been a question of moral economy: how should the economy and society be ordered? Moral economy introduces ideas of fairness, duties, rights, expectations, and entitlements, equality and liberty. In relation to the welfare state, the key issue is whether seeking to provide welfare through the state is a desirable or undesirable state of affairs. This issue has been debated throughout the history of modern political economy. Moral issues have always been inextricably linked with the development of the welfare state. If a particular set of institutions are seen as fair, then their legitimacy will be high and political support for them easier to mobilize. This is why arguments about the welfare state often take an explicitly moral form. At a time of economic and financial crisis, old stigmas and moral dividing lines are quickly revived. Since 2008, the traditional discourse of the deserving and undeserving poor has returned, only this time politicians distinguish between strivers and shirkers, or between makers and takers. Benefit cheats and benefit tourists are contrasted with families who are trying to do the right thing. The latter are entitled to their benefits but the former are not.

There are three important moral positions in relation to welfare and the desirability of welfare states: the socialist, the conservative, and the market libertarian. The first question which divides them is whether welfare should be provided collectively, and, if it should, whether that should be done by the state. The second question is how great the involvement of the state ought to be – what is the appropriate scope and scale of the welfare state? The answers given to these questions are not abstract, remote from the world of practice. The discourses on welfare have a powerful influence on events. They have a huge bearing on whether welfare states can survive the challenges they currently face. The ability to persuade citizens that welfare states should or should not exist is a crucial component in determining whether they will survive. Ideas matter, and key to welfare states are the contending ideas which define them.

The socialist case both for collective welfare and for a welfare state became one of the dominant ideas of the twentieth century. Socialists emphasize the need for solidarity based on mutual dependence, and argue that we have a moral obligation to share resources in communities in accordance with socially agreed criteria of fairness and need. Individuals are not free-standing. They depend for their existence and survival on communities. As members of those communities, they have a duty to contribute resources to help those less well off than themselves. Socialists have always placed the community above the individual. Individuals have rights and entitlements but only as members of communities. Redistribution of resources does not have to be through the state. As noted earlier, socialists were once extremely suspicious of the state because they saw it as the instrument of the propertied class which served their interests and not those of the wider community. The Israeli kibbutz is an example of a socialist community which redistributes resources and provides welfare for all its members without relying on a state bureaucracy to do so. The moral duty to serve the community and participate in its collective decision-making takes precedence over individual self-realization.

The problem with socialist experiments which do not rely upon the state is that they tend to be local and small-scale. Faced with the challenge of dealing with welfare in modern industrial urbanized societies, non-state coordination proved impractical, although there have been exceptions, such as the cooperative movement. But in the twentieth century the socialist case for welfare almost everywhere became a case for some form of welfare state. Forms of self-management were too partial and local. They could not match the universality and comprehensiveness which the modern state could supply. The practical advantages of using the state were obvious, once socialists had persuaded themselves that democracy had transformed the state and made it something they could use to achieve their goals. Although some socialists remained unreconciled to the state, the majority movements of the Left, the social democrats, all made their peace with it, and in time came to see it as essential. From being critics of the state, the socialists became its champions. One of the main reasons for this transformation was the development of the welfare state. Socialists realized they could build on the limited welfare states established by conservatives and liberals, using the enhanced capacities and tax-raising powers created during the world wars to introduce far-reaching universal programmes, involving substantial redistribution not only between generations but also between classes, relieving poverty and investing in citizens, creating a public sphere beyond the market.

The case for using the state in this way was not just practical, it was also moral. To make modern society a true community to which everyone contributed and from which everyone benefited, and in which extremes of poverty were overcome, meant making sure that everyone was treated the same. In a complex modern society, this could only be achieved through a central bureaucracy of the kind developed in many European states. Even liberal Victorian Britain developed new institutions like the Post Office. Under rules established in the mid-nineteenth century, the Post Office undertook to deliver letters anywhere in Britain for the same flat fee, rather than charging extra for distance or remoteness. All citizens were treated the same. This became the aspiration for the welfare state. Wherever citizens lived, they were entitled to the same service as everyone else. There should be no postcode lottery. A highly centralized state, once distrusted and opposed by socialists, became accepted as the best instrument for ensuring equal treatment and consolidating a sense of national citizenship. This universalism of the modern state, as the Germans and the French had already discovered, gave it potentially enormous reach and legitimacy. The state could act for the whole national community and become its embodiment.

The moral case for providing welfare collectively emphasizes the vulnerability of the majority of citizens to misfortunes and risks beyond their control – such as illness, unemployment, or incapacity. It appeals to the idea of solidarity: that those most able and fortunate have a duty to assist those in need or suffering misfortune. By pooling resources and risks, everyone can be helped at the point of their lives where they most need it. The state is an association of citizens who recognize their common fate and their common predicament, and allow the organized power of their association, the state, to act collectively on their behalf, collecting resources from citizens and redistributing them to those whose needs are most pressing. People's circumstances and inherited qualities vary enormously, and policies and institutions need to be developed to take proper account of them.[1]

In the socialist view, the moral basis of the welfare state is both equality and solidarity. But equality does not mean equality of outcomes; it means that everyone is treated the same by having the same entitlements and opportunities. The outcomes will be unequal not only because some citizens will earn more than others, but also because benefits will not be distributed equally. Those in greatest need will receive the most. Those who do not have children, or who never fall sick, or whose jobs are secure do not benefit as much from the welfare state as many others. But as Bo Rothstein has pointed out, they do benefit from living in a society in which every individual enjoys a basic security and opportunity to live a full life. In this way, everyone has a stake in the welfare state.[2]

From this standpoint, welfare, like defence, is a public good which the state should provide because the market either will not, or will not do so efficiently or sufficiently. Using taxes to redistribute income regardless of individual preferences is justified because the goal is to create a cohesive society from which everyone benefits. Clean air or safe drinking water may not emerge from the interplay of individual preferences. There will always be those for whom it is not a priority. But once achieved, everyone benefits, and very few would choose to give them up. This is the consequentialist argument. Many welfare policies are like this. A society with a developed welfare state and low levels of inequality and poverty is likely to promote trust, contentment, and social peace, all public goods which, once experienced, a society is not likely to want to surrender. But the case can also be stated in terms of first principles. A pattern of society in which every individual is provided with the means necessary for basic human dignity and flourishing is a society which conforms to universal principles of social justice. It is not a society in which there is equality of outcome or any attempt to create such equality, but it is a society in which there is substantial redistribution between classes and between generations.

The socialist case has been substantially extended in recent years by the incorporation of feminist and green perspectives. They have questioned some of the assumptions of the traditional socialist discourse and raised the key issue of sustainability. Earlier socialist and trade union ideas about welfare still emphasized the male breadwinner and the patriarchal household as the foundation of the welfare state. These attitudes shared much in common with the conservative perspective on welfare. One of the big changes in socialist thinking in the last four decades has been the recognition that the welfare state is seriously incomplete if it rests upon unpaid domestic labour to deal with problems such as unemployment, child care, social care, and old age. In the golden age of the welfare state, much welfare was still being provided through households, relying on a traditional division of labour between men and women. The key insight of feminist political economy is the priority it gives to the reproductive economy.[3] Ensuring the wider well-being of all members of households, reproducing people rather than just labour power, and investing in the services which free individuals from dependency on the market or the family are central to the feminist idea of a sustainable society. Greens further argue that the concept of well-being and sustainability needs to be extended to include the natural environment. A public sphere has to be built which can counter not only the impact of markets on the well-being of individuals in households but also damage to the ecosystems on which human life depends. The need in any political economy to understand the complex interaction between the state, markets, households, and the biosphere has only recently been fully understood. It has broadened the idea of the welfare state, extending its reach, but this in turn increases the challenges which welfare states face to deliver what they promise, and sharpens the dilemma of how to win support for an expanding not a contracting welfare state.

The conservative case for the welfare state is also a case which gives priority to the community over the individual, and particularly to the national community. Like socialists, conservatives are committed to forms of collective welfare and redistribution. It was conservative politicians who first made moves to institute state welfare provision, but once democracy was extended and socialists and other radical movements became advocates of state welfare, conservative support became much more qualified. Conservatives always emphasized the family and the household as the main site for welfare provision, and saw the state's role as providing support for families to discharge this role.

Conservative attitudes to welfare are rooted in paternalism, a desire to mitigate extreme poverty, and to allow families to have sufficient autonomy so that they can bring up the next generation and preserve key social values. There are deserving as well as undeserving families, and the difficulty for conservatives is to find ways to change the behaviour of the latter so that they conform to the model that conservatives value. This model has traditionally been the two-parent family, with the father as the main breadwinner and the mother as the main carer, both for children and for elderly relatives. This is regarded as a morally superior form of life.

In more recent times, many conservative parties have become more socially liberal, but traditional values are still strong in several countries, including parts of the United States. The conservative instinct is that social order depends on strong and stable families. If the welfare state undermines families, either by promoting a different model for bringing up children or by creating disincentives for people to get married, then that has harmful social consequences. A familiar conservative narrative is the broken society, where the family is undermined by permissiveness, divorce, teenage pregnancies, and welfare dependency. One of the most significant conservative discourses in relation to the welfare state has been that of Christian Democracy, which has drawn specifically on religious doctrines which stress the importance of community and the family.[4]

Conservatives were often the architects of the extended state of the twentieth century, particularly through their commitment to imperialism, nationalism, and war. They advocated strengthening defences to meet the challenge of rival powers, and this made them receptive to arguments for state spending not just to alleviate poverty and distress but also to increase the health and education of all citizens. The importance of manpower, both its quantity and its quality, became a major theme in conservative thinking. But although some of these conservatives were strong critics of laissez-faire individualism, they also did not want state powers pushed too far. In particular, they fiercely resisted the redistributive agenda of socialists where this began to encroach on the interests of property. Some conservatives worried about the gap between rich and poor, and advocated policies and institutions to create a common national citizenship, but they were not in favour of overturning existing hierarchies of power and wealth. They therefore came to argue against universalism becoming the core principle of welfare states, as socialists wanted. Instead, they stressed that there were many services which were best provided selectively, using means tests to restrict eligibility. The potentially limitless explosion of expectations and entitlements came to preoccupy conservatives and made them advocates of welfare state retrenchment to make it more manageable and affordable.

This is why in the neo-liberal era some conservatives have made common cause with market libertarians and other neo-liberals in seeking to roll back some of the gains of the era of high collectivism when welfare states appeared to be the wave of the future. But conservatives remain committed to a form of welfare state; in particular they are committed to strong and stable families and the relief of poverty, as well as to universal programmes of health and education. But their enthusiasm is limited. In the austerity programmes launched after 2008, conservative governments were at the forefront, putting financial stability and fiscal consolidation ahead of preserving entitlements and the level of welfare spending which had been built up in the previous ten years. Conservatives give increasing priority as well to delivering welfare through voluntary organizations rather than through the state. They are much less concerned than socialists with the unevenness of access to welfare, seeing variation as unavoidable and the attempt to treat people the same as imposing uniformity and requiring an unnecessary and damaging degree of centralization.

Socialists and conservatives prize different things about the welfare state, but both remain committed to a large part of welfare still being delivered through the state, funded by taxes, and therefore involving redistribution at least between groups at different stages of the life-cycle. The moral case for forms of collective welfare provision remains strong, whether the basic unit is the family, the nation, or the community. Organizing the state to redistribute resources and meet needs remains a shared moral commitment. The position for market libertarians is very different. Their moral position rejects the idea that some form of collective has a higher claim than the individual. For socialists and some conservatives, this position has often been seen as advocating selfishness, removing all restrictions on individual behaviour and the maximization of the interests of the individual regardless of the effects on others. Some extreme forms of market libertarianism do take this stance, although even here this is a position no less moral than that of socialists and conservatives.

Since the 1970s it has been the market libertarians who have argued most persistently that the welfare state should not survive, and some also believe that its many internal contradictions will lead to its demise. But here we are chiefly concerned with their moral argument. This argument was put most eloquently by Robert Nozick when he called for capitalism between consenting adults. Voluntary exchanges between free individuals are the basis of a free society. Any intervention by the state in those exchanges is coercive and harmful and should be either banned entirely or limited as much as possible. Nozick conceded a case for a minimal state to provide its citizens with law and order, but anything beyond this was illegitimate.[5] Specifically, he regarded any spending on welfare or redistributive taxation as an infringement on liberty. If individuals wished voluntarily to make payments to other citizens to enhance their welfare, that was a matter for them, but no-one should be coerced into doing so through taxation. Many market libertarians rejected even the argument that there was a role for the state in providing basic law and order, preventing people killing one another and stealing each other's property. But there was no case at all for providing welfare through the state. The state had no business being involved in whether individuals starved or not.

Such a view gives maximum moral weight to liberty, regarding restrictions on the liberty of the individual as inherently harmful. There is an egalitarianism at work here. All human beings are to be treated as equal, but the most important fact which makes them equal is their capacity for liberty. This is the rough equality of the state of nature as Hobbes described it. Equality of opportunity and equality of outcome arise as state projects of redistribution and as such have no place in a free society. On this view, the state has no more need to be providing welfare (whether health, education, pensions, or social security) than it has to be providing steel. Whatever the justifications for the welfare state in past societies, it is no longer needed in a properly constituted and functioning free market economy based on voluntary exchanges between sovereign individuals. Indeed, it is positively harmful, a major drag upon prosperity and growth because it has become wasteful and inefficient, and requires high levels of taxation to fund it. It is the last bastion of the command economy in Western societies, and it displays all the weaknesses of such an economy. Resources are misallocated; there is no proper market discipline or budget constraints. The welfare state has become a giant parasite on the rest of the economy, and threatens to suck the life out of the private sector, so insatiable is its appetite for additional resources.

The original idea that welfare programmes would be funded by individual national insurance contributions has been lost, and welfare programmes are now funded from general taxation. As costs, demands, and entitlements all rise, so does the need for additional resources to fund the welfare state. There is no end to this spiral, which threatens to capsize the public finances. It also politicizes welfare by empowering groups of claimants and public sector employees to push their special interests. Supporters of the welfare state are regarded as defenders of an increasingly indefensible status quo. The welfare state has become a serpent whose coils have fastened around the economy and the state and need to be prised off. Voters will increasingly vote for parties which promise to reduce the number of welfare dependants to a small core of citizens who genuinely cannot make provision for themselves. Similarly, voters will increasingly see the advantages to themselves of contracting for welfare as they contract for any other good or service, and paying much lower taxes in return. As privatization of health, education, and pensions takes hold, expectations will come back into line with resources, and a free economy and a minimal state will be restored, which will maximize the choice and quality of the services previously provided through the state.

As a doctrine, market libertarianism has strong utopian features and its full ideals have not so far been achieved anywhere. But it is a powerful and growing current in the politics of Western states. It sets out an alternative moral vision, arguing that the direction of policy should always be to reduce state spending and taxation so as to enlarge the sphere of individual liberty, self-realization, individual projects, and self-fulfilment. Individuals may choose to cooperate, but they should not be forced to do so.[6] This is a radical doctrine which challenges all forms of the extended state – spending on defence and arms as much as spending on welfare. It also challenges all interventions by the state which restrict human liberty, including drug laws, immigration controls, parenting classes, and compulsory education. Nations are collectives and have no higher moral authority to coerce individuals. If they arise spontaneously, they are compatible with liberty, but once they become instruments of states, liberty is lost.

Many of the challenges to the survival of the welfare state, whether in its conservative or socialist form, are now expressed in market libertarian language. The various strands of neo-liberalism are all heavily influenced by market libertarian ideas, although many of its currents allow a much greater role for the state, and even a role for the welfare state. Friedrich Hayek defended the idea that the state should guarantee a social minimum, a safety net to prevent extremes of poverty and destitution.[7] But even he offered a prudential rather than a principled argument. The social safety net was necessary to guard against the danger of revolution. It was a means to pacify and sedate the poor, a useful insurance policy to preserve the market order from social groups who might seek to destroy it.

The great moral and practical problem for market libertarianism is the same as it was for the classical liberalism of the nineteenth century: what to do about the poor. The ideal is that everyone should be self-reliant, independent, industrious, and self-contained. But what should then be done with those individuals who are not? Liberals, like conservatives, favoured certain forms of intervention, aimed at changing character and behaviour. Education has been a favoured liberal solution to social problems, reflecting an assumption that there is a rational core within every individual which can be released, permitting everyone to behave in ways which are consistent with a liberal order. No-one would be a charge on the state or the community. But progress towards this goal has always been slow, and in the meantime the liberal market order has had to deal with the poor, the feckless, the criminal, the idle, as well as the disabled, the old, and the very young. The moral dilemma of how to handle the poor, all those unable or unwilling to lead an independent life, was resolved in a number of ways, all of them familiar today. At the beginning of the industrial era, the Speenhamland system in England gave outdoor relief to the poor, but this was condemned as encouraging idleness and dependency, and was replaced in 1834 by the New Poor Law, which instituted a much harsher regime, refusing support to those able to fend for themselves, and herding everyone else into workhouses, where they were subject to a highly coercive regime and deprivation of liberty in return for bare subsistence.[8] Individuals placed in the workhouse lost their right to liberty, because they were no longer considered rational, independent individuals. Not all individuals were acceptable. They had to conform to a certain standard.

There is no place for the workhouse in the market libertarian utopia, but in the neo-liberal reality of contemporary societies the problem remains of what to do with the swelling numbers of the poor since the destruction of the full-employment economy of the post-war years and the destruction of so many skilled manufacturing jobs. In the austerity programmes imposed across Europe in the wake of the financial crash, the trend has been to punish the poor, steadily reducing the value of benefits and removing some benefits altogether, making it much harder for individuals to make claims, while forcing all citizens to bear more risks themselves. Welfare benefits grew in many countries in the upswing of the economy in the 1990s and the early 2000s, but now in the recession the public mood has changed. Support for certain parts of the welfare state has declined. This is particularly noticeable in relation to non-universal benefits such as social security.

The groups in receipt of social security are much more easily stigmatized as undeserving, and politically it has proved easier to squeeze the benefits of these groups. Survey evidence shows that most citizens believe that spending on, for example, benefits for the unemployed is a far higher proportion of the welfare budget than it is in reality.[9]

Fiscal squeezes at best contain the problem, and for market libertarians the goal is still to remove the problem altogether and get rid of the need to have any state-provided welfare at all. To achieve that they would need to broaden the attack beyond social security to the core universal programmes of the welfare state, such as health and education. The moral argument here is the same as with social security benefits. Welfare should be a matter of individual responsibility. Individuals should pay for the education of their children and should insure themselves against health risks or the risks of unemployment or disability. There is no reason why the state should be involved in the provision of either education or health for its citizens. These are private goods and can be left to the interaction between consumers and producers in free markets in the same way as any other good or service.

Progress towards this ideal has mostly been seen through the privatization of many delivery systems, allowing private companies to bid for public contracts, and slimming down public sector workforces. But states have retained control of funding, ensuring that the most important services are still free at the point of use. There have been experiments with vouchers and insurance, but they have run up against some severe practical difficulties. The moral question that arises when withdrawing the state entirely from provision or funding of education and welfare is what happens to those individuals not being covered by any insurance scheme, or who have insufficient cover for the treatments they need. The prevalence of low pay in neo-liberal economies, and the associated drive to take individuals at the bottom of the income scale out of tax makes it paradoxically very difficult to make all individuals responsible for their own health care and education. Those at the bottom of the income scale do not have any spare income to pay for the premiums and would not benefit from the cuts in income and capital taxes.

Conservatives are not committed to state solutions in either education or health, although they have often been ready to intervene in the curriculum or in public health issues. The interest of the national economy in having well-educated and healthy citizens justifies overriding the liberty of individuals. For conservatives, the issue is always how far they would allow either schools or hospitals to escape political control. The same is true for socialists. Both accept, in the way that market libertarians do not, that the nation or the community has a prior moral claim over the individual. In Ken Loach's film *The Spirit of '45* about the first majority British Labour government, there is the story of a family who had called the doctor to see a sick child. During the visit, the doctor hears another child coughing upstairs and asks to see him as well. The mother says she cannot afford the cost of the consultation, but the doctor explains that the service is now free, and she no longer has to have that anxiety. For socialists and many conservatives, stories like these justified the creation of welfare states. But for market libertarians, while they might sympathize with the particular case, there never can be justification for removing the liberty of individuals to make their own choices. Substituting the state for the individual leads inexorably to greater dependency.

The moral arguments around the welfare state have always come down to this. How desirable is it that the state should intervene in choices individuals make about their lives by requiring that children be educated, by imposing public health requirements, such as bans on smoking, and by using its coercive powers to extract revenue from citizens to fund redistributive welfare states? The balance of this argument is a key component in assessing whether or not the welfare state can survive. For much of the twentieth century, the moral argument was generally won by those arguing for extending state provision and reducing the risks and uncertainties individuals faced in their lives. But it has always been contested, and in recent decades the old laissez-faire liberalism of the nineteenth century has been reborn in the shape of contemporary market libertarianism, and has begun making inroads in many political parties and political systems across Europe. It challenges the reason for welfare states to continue to exist. Those who want welfare states to survive must meet these arguments head-on.

3

Four Challenges

The market libertarian tide has advanced and scored some successes, particularly in Anglo-America, but the political and social consensus in favour of sustaining a welfare state even in these countries has so far held. The social democratic welfare states in the Nordic countries and the conservative corporatist welfare state regimes in Western Europe have been most successful in resisting any trend towards 'de-commodification'. But even if this remains the case and majorities in all the Western democracies continue to want the welfare state to survive, there is no guarantee that it will. The new hard times ushered in by the financial crash have once again put the future of the welfare state in question. Will it pass the test again and find fresh ways to renew itself, or this time will it fall apart because the stresses placed upon it cause sufficient voters to withdraw support?

Four Challenges

The welfare state faces many challenges, but four are picked out here for closer analysis. They are interlocking, and to some extent have existed as long as welfare states have existed. But in their present form they are the products of the neo-liberal era, and reflect some of the key trends in the political economy of the last thirty-five years.

Affordability

This challenge is the one perhaps most often picked out as threatening the future of the welfare state. At its core is how to persuade people to pay higher taxes for the public services they say they want. Right from the beginning of the welfare state, there have always been fears that governments would promise too much or would make commitments they could not fulfil. The pressures on governments to spend more are intense, and in good times governments bend to those pressures and allow spending to rise. But this can mean that the amount governments are able to raise in taxes fails to keep pace with the amount they need to spend to cope with rising costs. This problem is particularly acute during recessions, but it exists at all times. Governments can deal with it by cutting back services, but this is unpopular.

Or they can look for efficiency savings, constantly reforming services in order to cut costs, but this can be slow. Or they can increase taxes or charges, but this too is unpopular. Or they can increase borrowing, but this encounters limits.

The problem is not really one of money. Western societies are much richer than when welfare states were first introduced. They could choose to spend more on welfare. Already there is a wide variation between what different states are willing to spend, with the Scandinavian social democracies tending to have the most generous welfare states and the highest taxes, and the Anglo-liberal states the least generous welfare states and the lowest taxes, with the conservative ordo-liberal states of the eurozone somewhere in the middle. The problem is one of political will. Voters in Western democracies vote for parties that promise them more spending on public services and lower taxes. They want Swedish-style public services and American-style taxes. Political parties pretend, with varying degrees of plausibility, to offer both. The acceptability of very high taxation has declined in many countries, as opportunities for personal consumption have mushroomed. As a result, politicians have become very wary of proposing new taxes, which always tend to be unpopular.

Four Challenges

If new taxes are hard to introduce, governments also find it increasingly difficult to increase existing taxes. In the neo-liberal era, parties increasingly compete with one another to promise not to raise the main forms of direct and indirect taxes – typically income taxes often deducted by employers on behalf of the state and sales taxes such as VAT. In recent years, governments across Europe and regardless of welfare regime have become interested in adopting fiscal rules which constrain their freedom of manoeuvre and commit them to strict targets on spending and borrowing to achieve fiscal surpluses.[1] In some instances, this also involves laws to prevent governments increasing certain taxes. The resilience of such rules has yet to be properly tested. Many observers assume that if a financial emergency was grave enough, any government would suspend such rules to raise taxes and would have no compunction in doing so. After the 2008 financial crash, all Western governments were willing to adopt extraordinary measures to prevent the economy going into freefall.

The political enthusiasm in the neo-liberal era for much stricter fiscal rules and fiscal surpluses reflects an expectation fostered by politicians of all parties that tax rates should never rise but only come down. When tax rates are increased, it is understood that this is temporary and will be reversed as soon as possible. This is very different from tax regimes in the past, when it was accepted that in periods of financial emergency tax rates needed to be increased to restore fiscal balance. In the neo-liberal era, at least as far as the Anglo-liberal states are concerned (the ordo-liberal states of the eurozone are a different matter), there are really no fiscal conservatives left in the traditional sense. In denying themselves the ability to raise taxes, they have to put all the emphasis on reductions in spending, often politically a much harder task. To get round this difficulty, governments have become adept at promoting stealth taxes. These are taxes which have a low public profile. The most useful stealth tax of all in the past was fiscal drag, the process by which inflation pushed taxpayers into higher tax brackets without any political decision from governments. One of the problems of the neo-liberal era is that inflation has declined to very low levels, and in many countries there is now greater pressure towards deflation rather than inflation.[2] The benefits of fiscal drag are as a result much reduced, and governments in many countries, such as Japan, are seeking to raise the rate of inflation not lower it.

This downward pressure on tax rates extends to pressure for removing certain kinds of taxation altogether. This is most evident in the fiscal competition which sees states compete with one another to lower taxes on capital, and also to tolerate tax arrangements for the rich which allow them to avoid high tax burdens. In the United States there is pressure to abolish inheritance tax permanently, and there has also been interest in the US and in some Eastern European countries in the idea of flat taxes: abolishing all forms of progressivity in the tax system, and requiring instead individuals to pay a fixed proportion of their income, say 20 per cent, or even a fixed amount. Both would be highly regressive, and would be designed to entrench a permanently lower level of tax revenue from which government would have to fund its spending, including spending on the welfare state.

Market libertarians have long been fascinated with curves which purport to show a relationship between tax rates and tax yields and also between tax rates and economic growth. The Laffer curve in the 1980s was invoked to provide substance to the trickle-down thesis: the claim that reducing tax rates on the rich would actually increase tax revenues because the rich would stop finding ways to shield so much of their income from the tax authorities. The evidence for this was always highly dubious. The main effect of lowering tax rates on the rich and reducing the progressivity of the tax system was dramatically to increase inequality. More recently, the Cato Institute has championed the Rahn curve, which attempts to show that there is an optimum level for government spending if the aim is to maximize economic growth.[3] This is calculated to be between 15 and 20 per cent of national income. If it goes above this (and among advanced economies only a few special cases such as Hong Kong are below), then economic growth will be much lower. Among the Western economies, public spending (a large part of which is spending on the welfare state in one form or another) varies from 35 per cent to 50 per cent. But there is no obvious correlation with economic growth. Some of the highest spenders, such as the Scandinavian economies, have had persistently high growth rates. There is considerable evidence that strong welfare states boost economic growth rather than hold it back.[4]

But although the economic argument fails, the political argument is still potent, because lower taxes is what many voters want, so long as it is other people's services which are cut. This race to the bottom in the Western tax states means that they come to suffer from a chronic shortage of revenue to fund public services. This makes the welfare state always look unaffordable, always on the edge of a new financial crisis. In the United States, the Republicans in Congress in recent years have been firmly opposed to any new taxes on the wealthy and advocate only spending reductions to deal with the ballooning US national debt. (It had reached $18 trillion in 2015 – six times the debt Ross Perot was so worried about in 1992.) Paul Ryan, who, as noted in chapter 1, became the Republican nominee for Vice President in the 2012 US presidential election, put forward the Ryan Plan for achieving budget balance. It proposed reducing the federal budget to around 15 per cent of US national income by 2050. The Congressional Budget Office calculated that the effect of the plan would be massive cuts in federal spending programmes.

Barack Obama's re-election in 2012 means that there has been no attempt as yet to implement anything approaching the Ryan Plan in the United States. But it forms part of a pattern of persistent agitation by market libertarians in the US for amendments to the Constitution to entrench a fiscal regime of permanently balanced budgets and low taxation. Such a regime, if ever achieved, would make the preservation of even a residual welfare state very difficult. Nor is this debate limited to the United States. Canada has already introduced a Federal Balanced Budget Act, and the United

Kingdom's Charter for Budget Responsibility commits governments to budget surpluses when the economy is growing. The battles over levels of taxation are crucial for the survival of the welfare state. Any state which cannot collect taxes is close to collapse, unable to function. The same is true of welfare states. If tax resistance and tax evasion reach certain levels so that either taxes cannot be collected in sufficient amounts (as in Greece) or taxes cannot be increased above a certain level, this severely limits what kind of welfare state, if any, is possible. Research on willingness to pay shows that the sustaining of broad political coalitions is essential. If all citizens benefit from welfare programmes at some point in their lives, they are more likely to support the taxation necessary to fund the welfare state.[5]

The other side of affordability is spending. One of the reasons why the right libertarian agenda has not advanced as far as its protagonists hoped is that although many voters are increasingly keen on seeing taxes reduced, they also do not want spending on services to be reduced. On the contrary, they want it to rise, or at the very least they want the quality of services to be maintained. With declining tax revenues, this is an impossible circle to square. Governments try to do so by offering to protect and ringfence the services which are valued most, or at least which are valued by a majority of voters, or by voters who actually vote. This means that it is the universal programmes on health, education, and pensions which tend to get protected. In the austerity programmes of Europe, the interests of pensioners have been safeguarded in almost all states, which reflects the fact that they are much more likely to vote than younger citizens. Similarly, health and education are services which the vast majority rely on and which still have high levels of approval. The areas of spending which are targeted are those which benefit minorities: the disabled, the unemployed, and low-income working families. As noted in the previous chapter, these benefit recipients can much more easily be stigmatized than can pensioners, or than those who use the schools and hospitals. It is here generally where the axe falls. Sympathy for welfare spending which supports the poor has declined. Popular attitudes support welfare spending where there is a contributory principle; but there is much less support for those programmes where no contribution is made.

When austerity really bites, however, as it has in Greece, some of these rules get broken, but that is because the government loses its sovereignty. The Syriza government in Greece insisted that protecting pensioners was one of its red lines, a pattern seen across Europe. Funding pensioners actually protects many other groups, including the unemployed young, because resources get redistributed through households. But in the last-ditch renegotations over a new bailout in June 2015 Greece's creditors, the Troika of the European Central Bank, the European Union, and the International Monetary Fund refused to accept the government's proposals for increases in corporate taxation and taxation on the rich, believing that these taxes could not be collected, and instead proposed further cuts to pensions, including the poorest pensioners, whom Syriza had vowed to protect. In fiscal squeezes in the neo-liberal era, the default position both in Anglo-liberal capitalism and in ordo-liberal capitalism has been to cut spending and not taxes, and in Greece and several other ordo-liberal countries this has meant cuts in core programmes. In Anglo-liberal countries, the cuts have been severe but so far have been concentrated in programmes that do not directly affect the majority.

The other way of avoiding deep spending cuts but also to avoid large tax increases is to deliver efficiencies. Public service reform is not new. It has always been part of the welfare state, but since the crisis of the 1970s it has acquired a new urgency.[6]

The recognition that mature welfare states exhibited a constant tendency for spending to increase faster than the resources available to sustain them inspired constant efforts to restructure the welfare state, reforming its operations and subjecting it to new disciplines and targets, in a bid to enhance efficiency, raise productivity, and slow the inexorable rise in costs. Any mature welfare state that was not being constantly reformed would probably not survive very long. The problem is not whether efficiency savings are possible but whether they are ever enough to contain rising costs and meet rising expectations.

The neo-liberal era gave an extra twist to this debate through the development of what became known as the new public management, with its emphasis on targets, audits, quasi-markets, the split between purchasers and providers, and experiments with contracting out and novel forms of financing, such as the public finance initiative. What the new public management sought to do was to allow managers to measure output and performance more precisely, and to use these measures to improve productivity and efficiency.[7] Controversy abounds as to how far these methods were successful, or whether they mainly added another level of bureaucracy, which then in its turn became a target for culling.

The professionals who used to run services were pushed aside and subordinated to the new public service managers, who now became a recognized stratum in every advanced welfare state. Their function was to be engaged in continual reform of the services they were managing and regulating.

The affordability dilemma in the neo-liberal era has arisen from both the desire of voters to have lower taxes, or at least not higher taxes, and at the same time the desire of the same voters to have better and more services. This is one of the reasons why governments of all political persuasions embraced the language of perpetual reform which the new public management offered them. Another reason was that welfare states did not just satisfy demands from voters, they are also integral to modern political economies, their reproduction and sustainability. It helps explain why even radical governments influenced by market libertarians have made relatively little progress in dismantling the welfare state either in the good times or now in the bad times of the neo-liberal era. There has not yet been the kind of step-change to a much reduced size of state which would be needed to realize the market libertarian agenda.

One of the reasons for this is the rising tide of expectations and the entitlements which go with them. Welfare states can seem quite affordable if entitlements are kept limited. At the beginning of welfare states, the goals were extremely modest: the provision of a basic pension for old age, and social security to cover risks arising from unemployment and ill health. But the needs of the economy and the pressures of competitive democratic politics have transformed that. Modern citizenship has been built on making civil, political, and social rights truly universal,[8] and that has meant uncovering the multiple sources of inequality and discrimination against particular groups. Since the ideal of the welfare state is to achieve full self-realization for all its citizens, the best way to ensure this is by recognizing that every individual citizen should be entitled to enjoy certain goods, have access to certain opportunities, and be protected against certain harms. As societies get richer, so the quality threshold in providing entitlements rises. Should welfare states provide only the basics, or should they strive to make available the best that there is? Here is the dilemma. If they do the former, then they provide little more than a basic safety net, and inequality will persist, because families which can afford to will purchase the highest-quality education and health care. If they do the latter, they open Pandora's box, because the quality of what can be provided is always rising and so is the expense. To provide the best health service possible, there need to be constant increases in the resources made available to it, and that means either charges for specific services or higher taxes.

The problem lies in universal benefits, since by their nature they tend to be potentially open-ended. There has long been a debate in welfare states about the merits of universalism over selectivity, a distinction highlighted by Richard Titmuss.[9] If benefits or services are made selective, they can be directed to those who need them the most, while withheld from those who can afford to do without them. Selectivity certainly reduces the costs of welfare programmes if eligibility rules are tight enough and enforced. But there are disadvantages too. They involve some kind of means test, which imposes costs of its own and is often very bureaucratic. Means tests attract a stigma, and many people who ought to claim prefer not to, both because of the stigma and because of the hassle. Universal benefits have the great merit that since they are available to all citizens, there is no stigma in accepting them. They are an entitlement. They are also essential if there is to be broad-based political support for an extended welfare state.

Conservatives and market libertarians have always worried about an entitlement culture because it tends to set expectations of what the state should deliver on a rising curve, severing the link between outputs and costs. In earlier periods, governments dealt with this problem by asserting the primacy of fiscal balance, and imposing financial caps on the money available for any particular benefit. Either that benefit then has to be rationed or its value has to be reduced. This can lead to harsh politics. In fiscal squeezes in the early decades of the welfare state, orthodox financial doctrine decreed that budgets must be balanced by raising taxes, reducing expenditure, or increasing borrowing.[10] The second was always the favoured route, and finance ministries were quite ready to cap spending even on open-ended benefits such as unemployment benefit. Balancing the budget took precedence over any item of current expenditure. That included citizens' entitlements.

Those fiscal doctrines were largely abandoned in the post-war Keynesian era. When they resurface, as they have done during the Greek crisis, it comes as a shock. The Greeks were asked by their creditors to cut entitlements, including pensions, in order to restore fiscal balance. In most other countries where governments are under such duress, there are strong incentives to avoid any such direct confrontation on universal entitlements. They may be weakened, for example by raising the age at which pensions are paid, but such changes are generally phased in over long periods, and care is taken not to affect the interests of current pensioners. In several countries, even during the implementation of austerity, certain universal benefits and programmes have been specifically protected, and in some cases their position has even been enhanced.

When the numbers are rolled forward, the financial commitments of some of the big universal entitlements which have come to characterize the welfare state can seem alarming. The United States is reckoned to have amassed unfunded entitlements amounting to $61 trillion in pensions and Medicare. Given the deadlock in Congress between Republicans and Democrats over raising taxes, the country faces a debt burden that will continue to grow. The United States is very wealthy and could eliminate its debts by choosing to raise taxes. But as long as that political option is blocked, the US budget continues to be adrift. The problem is passed on to the next generation to solve, along with climate change and much else. The United States is not known for the generosity of its welfare state, but its commitment to some core entitlements, such as Medicare and pensions, which are extremely popular, even among Tea Party supporters, makes it an exemplar of what can go wrong with welfare states when entitlements and expectations exceed the political capacity to fund them.

The revolution of entitlements has been one of the great changes of the last hundred years, associated with the rise of democratic citizenship and the expanding horizons which this has encouraged. One of the key areas where this has manifested itself is in the household, the sphere of gendered division of labour and social reproduction. The household has always played a vital role in the provision of welfare. It is a collective institution and acts to absorb many of the problems and deal with many of the risks created by market economies. When welfare states contract, it is generally families which must step in to fill the gap, and within families it is most often women who perform that role, in terms of care of children, the elderly, the disabled, and the sick. Capitalism has always depended on non-market institutions to be viable; households were for a long time the crucial support, and in many countries still are. Gradually that role was taken over by welfare states, and women were emancipated to pursue lives on a more equal basis with men. But whenever there is a fiscal crisis and a new bout of austerity, the state suddenly starts shovelling responsibilities back on to families.

Four Challenges

The entry of many more women into the labour force has had major economic as well as social benefits, but the battle to ensure that there is equal and fair treatment between men and women is far from won, in part because of the hidden support which is still required from families and the voluntary sector, which is again disproportionately staffed by women. The gradual extension of child care and nursery provision, specific income support through child benefits, carers' allowances, and improvements generally to social care and provision for the disabled – all this is essential if the unequal nature of domestic labour is not to reassert itself whenever a new financial crisis hits. There has been some progress, but there is still a long way to go. In this area of the welfare state, as in so many others, the appetite for more state provision, once aroused, becomes hard to satisfy within existing financial constraints. But it creates a body of support for extending the coverage of the welfare state and the quality of the services it can deliver. Welfare states are often depicted by their critics as forever spiralling into black holes of debt and waste, and this is given as the reason why they will not survive. They cannot control their costs. But welfare states which do best, such as those in Scandinavia, manage to achieve both increasing quality of services and deeper engagement with citizens' needs, while at the same time generating the political consent for the gathering of the resources which keep them solvent. It can be done.

International competitiveness

The second key challenge facing contemporary welfare states and governments seeking to manage them is how to maintain a welfare state in an open economy. After several decades in the twentieth century when international monetary cooperation collapsed, trade stagnated or shrunk, and protectionism in all its forms advanced, the period since 1945 saw a gradual opening of the international economy once again, with the establishment of a new international monetary order, and steady efforts to liberalize the movement of goods, capital, and even people. After the 1970s and the neoliberal turn executed by the United States and the United Kingdom, the pace of opening quickened. The new monetary and fiscal rules developed to counter inflation were accompanied by the steady abandonment of capital controls, the floating of currencies, the opening of borders, and the freeing of trade. These trends were enhanced by the end of the Cold War and the division of the world into two separate economic and military blocs.

The new opening acquired a new name, globalization, and although the claims for it were often exaggerated, it did represent a marked shift from the earlier post-war period, and still more from the inter-war period and the world wars themselves. This was much more like a return to the liberal international order over which Britain had presided in the nineteenth century. One important difference was that there were no colonial empires left. The new phenomenon since the 1990s has been the emergence of a group of rising powers, among them China, India, and Brazil. These powers with their vast populations began to grow rapidly, transforming the nature of the international economy, its division of labour, and the prospects for its future governance. These developments suggested that during the twenty-first century there would be a significant change in the balance of the international economy, with much greater weight and political power accruing to the rising powers.

The remarkable progress of the rising powers was a key factor in the long economic upswing which began in the 1990s and lasted, with some interruptions, until the financial crash of 2008. The rising powers contributed low-cost manufactures which now flooded the markets of the Western economies, lowering inflation and boosting living standards. But what they also did was raise anxieties about where the process would stop. In the new division of labour of the international economy, how would the Western economies readjust to survive? As more and more manufacturing and service jobs were outsourced to the rising powers, many worried that it would be hard to find replacement jobs for the workers who were displaced. If jobs could not be found for them, many might become dependent on welfare benefits, requiring an increase in spending and therefore a further shortfall in resources to pay for it.

The Western economies seemed to be caught in a bind. It was difficult to reverse globalization and the liberalization of the international economy with which it was associated. But if the wages and labour standards in the rising powers were so much lower than in Europe and the United States, there was little that could be done to prevent the loss of jobs. The only remedy might be to lower wages and labour standards in the advanced economies so as to be able to compete. Such moves would be very difficult politically, not least because it would require not just action on wages, but also action on the social wage. One of the reasons why Western

workers were no longer competitive with workers from poor countries was because they were
supported by a dense network of welfare benefits
and entitlements. Strip all that away, some market
libertarians argue, and Western workers could price
themselves back into jobs.

The core of this argument is that much of the
wealth and the enhancement of that wealth through
the social wage in the Western economies has been
in part due to the way these economies have been
protected in the last hundred years, but particularly
in the forty years after 1945 when a liberal international market order was being re-established.
Western economies had a privileged structural position in the international economy which they used
to build their wealth and entrench it. Enhancing
the social wage through an expanded welfare state
which brought domestic peace and a large internal
market was one of the main fruits of this.

With the advent of the era of globalization,
however, this post-war settlement came under
attack. Many of the jobs are no longer competitive
internationally and disappear, while there is growing pressure from economic migrants to enter the
wealthy countries. The twentieth-century welfare
states were always projects of nation-states. The
community in which resources were to be shared

and redistributed was always a national one. Many programmes were universal, but they were universal within national spaces. There were a few eccentrics who thought about world government and world distribution, but this was never likely to be practical politics. The discrepancy can be seen in the amounts states typically spend on their welfare budgets and the amount they dispense in foreign aid. The UN development target for foreign aid is 0.7 per cent of national income. Few states achieve this. But they will spend 20 per cent or more on welfare programmes for their own citizens.

This is another paradox at the heart of modern welfare states. They were developed to mitigate the extreme inequality and insecurity which laissez-faire capitalism generated. They succeeded in taming capitalism and creating social democracies in which the majority came to enjoy not just civil and political but also social rights. In the second half of the twentieth century, this made these economies rich and stable. In the era of globalization, however, they have become not only a magnet for the poor of the world, who try to enter them to find work, but also at the same time uncompetitive with the new forms of laissez-faire capitalism arising in Asia, which are unencumbered by employment rights or the cost of state-provided welfare. The Western welfare states become little oases of prosperity and harmony, and to preserve their privileges populist movements increasingly demand restrictions on immigration and restrictions on trade.

Global competition threatens the survival of the welfare state if welfare comes to be seen as a luxury which can no longer be afforded. This is a refrain often heard from market libertarians, but sometimes on the social democratic left as well. There are often calls for costs to be reduced to make Western workers competitive again, and warnings about 'the global race' and how the wealth and employment of the Western economies are not guaranteed. However, even if all welfare costs funded through the state were stripped out, Western workers would still not be competitive with workers in China, Vietnam, and Indonesia. To be competitive, Western economies have to move up the value chain, using skills, networks, and accumulated capital to develop new products and services which cannot be replicated by cheap labour in other parts of the world. But that would require increasing investment in education and training, which, since they are unlikely to be financed by private corporations, must be financed by the state. To keep the economy competitive and citizens in employment requires major long-term investment by the state in human capital. This enlarges the welfare state rather than contracts it, with all the implications for funding which then arise. Stripping out the welfare state would damage employment and prosperity in the Western economies.

This is a familiar pattern in the history of welfare states. If the welfare state was just about relief of poverty and suffering, welfare spending might be sacrificed were this the only way to price workers into jobs. But if the only way to price workers into jobs is to invest in them, to give them the skills to perform different kinds of jobs, then cutting back the welfare state will only create bigger problems for state budgets further down the line. At the same time, most Western economies have found it very hard to make the social investment strategies work for all their people. Too many remain long-term unemployed, with low skills and employability and therefore dependent on benefits. Employers are naturally attracted to the large numbers of young, highly motivated, highly skilled immigrants who are willing to come and do a wide range of jobs in the economy. But this then creates social and political tensions in many communities, over jobs, housing, schools, and the cultural integration of the newcomers.

Four Challenges

These are intractable problems, but welfare states are learning to survive them. What is important is not to retreat into narrow forms of protectionism.[11] There are limits to the amount of immigrants any community can absorb if the flow is too high, but provided the flow can be controlled, welfare states have shown themselves capable of helping to build diversified but also integrated communities. Austerity programmes can, however, put all this progress at risk if they destroy trust and increase insecurity, and also threaten the future affordability of welfare states if they lead to cutbacks in social investment which is so important in creating the high-skilled, high-paid jobs and individuals the future economy will need, at the same time placing arbitrary restrictions on the flow of migrants. Getting the balance right is enormously complex, and given the crude way in which issues such as welfare benefits and immigration are discussed in the media, politicians continually appear on the defensive. But there is no real alternative. The gains which welfare states represent should not be thrown away. At the same time, they cannot be protected by turning Europe into a fortress against the rest of the world. Efforts to increase aid and the pace of development around the world are the only sure long-term remedies.

Four Challenges

New social risks

The third key challenge is the emergence of a set of new social risks, alongside those which the welfare state was originally introduced to tackle. These new social risks are associated with the transition from a manufacturing economy to a service economy, and the emergence of a more individualist society and political culture, of which neo-liberalism is one manifestation. The political challenge for defenders of the welfare state is how to make the case for solidarity in such a climate. Many of the institutions which spontaneously supported collectivism and collectivist attitudes in the past have been weakened or destroyed. They include trade unions, mass-production factories, close-knit working-class communities, churches, and extended families. This is not a new trend. It is inscribed in the logic of the development of capitalism as an economic and social order. Individuals have been set free from the collective bonds of nation, community, and family. This has given individuals much greater personal liberty and private space, much more room for experiment and projects of self-creation; it has made them more independent and self-reliant, and less keen to accept dictates of authority, whatever their source.

Four Challenges

The new social risks are centred on new emerging patterns of work, households, and dependency.[12] Key developments have been: the much higher levels of participation of women in the workforce; the creation of a far larger group of citizens permanently dependent on benefits; the growth of single-parent families; the increase in job insecurity with the shrinking of permanent well-paid jobs and the growth of part-time, temporary, minimum-wage jobs; the growing importance of social care in an ageing population; the trend for increasing numbers of workers to be trapped by only possessing low skills or skills which have become obsolete; and the inadequacy of social provision against many of these risks. Some of these risks would previously have been handled by extended families, but changes in family structure make this less likely. Many of the groups affected by the new social risks are marginalized and lack the kind of networks and capacities to mobilize in support of new rights. Social democratic parties are most sensitive to the needs of these groups, but other groups are much better organized politically. Those most affected by the new social risks tend to be more isolated and fragmented and less able to make their needs count. Many of them do not vote.

These trends have created both obstacles and opportunities for welfare states. They have made spontaneous, unreflective solidarity less common. There has been increased pressure for individuals to become autonomous financial agents, taking responsibility for choices and decisions at every stage of the life-cycle once they become adult. This involves taking on increasingly large debts to navigate the life-cycle, such as student loans, mortgages, and pensions, as well as many different kinds of insurance. In addition, individuals increasingly borrow in order to buy immediately the goods and services they want. Financial services have expanded to fill the demand that these needs create. The mushrooming of credit cards, personal loans, long-term finance, online banking, and financial products for every possible life-choice and life-risk has become an everyday reality for most citizens.

The way in which welfare states are funded and organized runs counter to most of these trends. Citizens pay a significant proportion of their incomes in taxes, either directly or indirectly, and services are provided often in a top-down way, with limited possibility of citizen involvement, participation, or choice. The old command economy model of the welfare state drew on military modes of organization, and tended to concentrate power and decision-making in the hands of experts, managers, and professionals. There was an emphasis on hierarchy, discipline, and efficiency. At their best when directed to the achievement of a single goal, command models of organization can be highly effective, but they increasingly clashed with the desire of citizens to exercise more choice and control over the decisions which affected them. The challenge for welfare states has been whether they are able to introduce some of the flexibility and responsiveness to their customers that is characteristic of supermarkets.

The defenders of traditional models of the welfare state argue that the services and products which welfare states provide are quite unlike those provided by supermarkets. Good health and education are too important to be subject to market exchange as though they were just commodities which can be bought and sold like soap. One of the distinctive arguments for the welfare state has been that it is a sphere which recognizes that there are some goods which should not be commodities, and which should be provided in a way that is different from markets. This gives a large role to professionals, those with expert knowledge, to determine what a particular welfare good consists in and how it should be provided, and to whom. If citizens have trust in professionals to make the right decisions in the light of the best evidence, then this is a system which works well. But one of the consequences of the rise of a more individualist exchange and contract-oriented culture is that the market invades more and more spheres of social life, and individuals want more control over the decisions and choices which affect them. They lose trust in professionals to make the decisions for them. Various scandals in welfare states around the world, particularly in the medical sphere, but also in child protection and education, have caused trust in professionals to weaken, and have made citizens much more assertive.

As a result, there have been increasing experiments with new models of organization for welfare states. Some of these involve the direct participation of citizens in the governance of the services they use. But there are always problems of ensuring representativeness and efficient decision-making. The more common reforms have been to introduce markets or quasi-markets into welfare services, treating citizens as though they were consumers. Real markets involve lowering barriers to entry and allowing many different producers to compete for customers. But the prospect of unlicensed deregulated markets operating in health or education has generally been a step too far for most governments. Besides, they would only work if governments were prepared to take the further step of no longer letting the state provide or purchase services on citizens' behalf, but radically reducing taxation and leaving it up to individuals how they choose to spend their money.

The logic of a more individualist society, where everyone has become a financial agent and learnt to manage their assets and debts, and to calculate risks and returns, is clearly against the ethos and purpose of collectivist institutions like the welfare state. Advocates of public service reform argue that citizens will not be satisfied if public services do not offer them the kind of choice and flexibility which they have become used to in so many other markets. If individuals have increasing control in other parts of their economic affairs, why should they not be given the same freedom within the welfare state? Opponents say that this is an agenda for full privatization. Once there is a split between purchasers and providers of services, with providers becoming mostly private for-profit companies, the next logical step is to remove the state as a purchaser, transferring that role to individual citizens.

No government has actually gone this far yet. There remain strong reasons for not doing so. Whether or not to remove the state from the provider role has often been controversial, but it does not in principle breach the idea of services provided through the taxpayer and free at the point of use. Many countries allow a range of organizations – both not-for-profit and for-profit – to provide services. There are serious issues about whether the taxpayer gets a good deal, and the extent to which public resources are siphoned off into private profits without any real gain in service quality. But the basic principle of collective provision remains. Transferring the purchasing role to individuals would entail full privatization, and a major shake-up of taxation and spending. Some regulation would probably be imposed to prevent major scandals, although market libertarians such as Milton Friedman have long argued that the best form of regulation is competition.[13] Bad and fraudulent producers will not survive because consumers will vote with their feet and boycott them. The main practical objection to this policy is that the market would make a correction only after quite a lot of people had suffered serious harm.

How big a challenge is the spread of greater individualism to the welfare state? If all citizens were to embrace a market libertarian ethic, accepting in full the risks of living in a commercial society, then the appetite for either paying the existing level of taxes to support welfare provision or allowing choices and decisions to be made for them would quickly become intolerable and political parties would start to campaign on programmes to dismantle the welfare state. The rise of individualism certainly has influenced the growth of resistance to increased taxes, and has helped undermine the legitimacy of welfare states, and the instinctive support for them. There has been a weakening of political support for collective solutions to social problems, with some key groups in democratic electorates now opposed to increases in taxes to fund collective services. It is particularly noticeable how a division has opened up in many Western societies between private sector and public sector workers, with the latter being much more ready to support continuing high levels of public spending, not simply because they benefit from it but also because they believe in the public ethos and a strong public realm, as a counter to the individualist ethos of the market.

But the agenda of market libertarians has not made greater progress because the desire of citizens for greater personal freedom and independence is balanced by their desire for greater security. Most citizens remain risk averse, which is reflected in many of the products the financial services offer. There is also an increasing desire for greater government regulation of all kinds of matters throughout society, including the family. The reach of government in the neo-liberal era has been advancing not retreating when the number of areas in which government is expected to intervene is taken into account, from food labelling to smoking to transport. Fundamental areas like health, education, housing, and pensions show the same desire. Citizens want to know that they are safe, and when things go wrong they blame the government for not regulating the offending sector toughly enough. This was true even of the financial crash itself. The banks were blamed for their behaviour, but so too were governments for not regulating the banking sector in such a way that the excesses which led to the crash were prevented.

The modern individual is a curious amalgam of qualities in which different principles contend for mastery. More individuals have been obliged to become financial agents to a greater extent than ever before in the history of our modern commercial societies. In such societies, everyone is a merchant, as Adam Smith observed, but relatively few enjoy exposure to risk and many seek protection from it. If that is so in relatively unimportant areas of life, it is even more so in those areas which are central to any notion of human flourishing and well-being. These are the areas typically covered by welfare states. So long as they still discharge that function, most citizens are unlikely to vote for the dismantling of the protection it offers them. The problem is perhaps a more insidious one. It is the way greater individualism can make citizens less attentive to the needs of others, less convinced of the need for solidarity with those who are not as well off as they are, less willing to pay the taxes needed to keep universal protection in place. There is evidence particularly in the recent recessions in the Western economies of some hardening of attitudes towards the poor, with those claiming benefits viewed unsympathetically. Does this mean that the acceptance of the need for redistribution is declining? Or that there is now a much greater tolerance of inequality in Western societies? Rising inequality is a fact which will be discussed in the final chapter, but the evidence as to whether there is greater tolerance of it is mixed, in part because there is only limited understanding of the extent of the inequality which is once more emerging.

Welfare states can survive some erosion of the support for redistribution and for collective solutions, but it weakens them, and makes them appear ponderous and persistently ailing. This is why reforming public services remains important. Reconciling a more individualist culture and the concomitant expectations of service standards and product standards is as important for the welfare state as for any other organization. But what has to be avoided is following managerial agendas which talk the language of customer care and customer satisfaction but in practice are insulated from the actual concerns of those using public services. Getting that relationship right is vital to ensure the long-term survival of welfare states. But it is a complex matter. After several decades of reform, many familiar complaints are still heard, and shortcomings are still exposed. There is probably no escape from this.

Ageing

A fourth challenge is demographic: the problems of ageing and fertility and how they can affect the sustainability and legitimacy of welfare states. One of the most important aspects of welfare states is the way in which they redistribute resources between the generations, guaranteeing to everyone in old age sufficient income to live on, and appropriate health care and social care. Dignity in retirement has long been an aim of welfare states, and pensions were one of the first programmes to be developed. The need to support people when they were no longer able to work or were ready to retire from work was obvious and widely accepted. Redistribution of resources from young people to old people became part of a social contract in which individuals understood that they would contribute now, and their contributions would fund retired citizens, and that in return they would receive support from younger citizens when it was their turn to retire.

Such a model worked well, but it did depend on there being a steady supply of young workers to take the places of the ones who reached the age of retirement. It also assumed that the usual pattern would be for the flow of those entering the workforce to be greater than the flow of those retiring. Otherwise there might not be enough younger workers to support the aged population. Another assumption was expectations of mortality. In the Beveridge Report, published in 1942, which provided a road map for the much-expanded welfare state constructed in Britain after 1945, the pension age was fixed at 65 for men and 60 for women, reflecting the relatively small number of citizens expected to live much beyond that age. Many of these assumptions have been confounded by later developments. In most Western societies, there has been a pronounced deceleration of the rate of population growth. There has also been a significant increase in life expectancy, a striking success of the welfare state and its social investment in people. The result has been that many Western societies have experienced an ageing population, with the proportion of elderly people steadily increasing. In some countries, such as Italy and Japan, demographic trends point to the population shrinking.

Such trends are a problem for welfare states because they imply that extra resources must be extracted from a relatively declining pool of younger workers in order to maintain the value of pensioner benefits. There are many ways of alleviating the problem, which is also one of intergenerational fairness, but none of them are very popular. The easiest, on which most countries have made a start, is to restrict eligibility for pensions by raising the state pension age, not just once but progressively in line with the rise in life expectancy. A second option is to reduce the generosity of state pension benefits, but this is difficult because of the power of the pensioner lobby and still more of the pensioner vote. In all the democracies, pensioners wield considerable political influence because, as noted above, they are more likely to vote than younger citizens. In all the established democracies during the austerity programmes of recent years, it is noticeable how pensioner rights have tended to be protected. Sometimes pensions and pensioner benefits have been explicitly ringfenced, and pensioners given guarantee of a real-terms increase much more generous than anything being offered to younger workers. Such crude tactics have often paid off. In the United Kingdom, where pensions and pensioner benefits had been one of the areas ringfenced from austerity, the grey vote swung decisively to the Conservatives in the 2015 general election.

A third alternative is to stimulate the birth rate. In the 1950s, the French went to great lengths to increase the birth rate by offering a range of financial incentives to anyone who conceived. The programme had some success but only for a time. There would be much more difficulty in imposing these incentives in today's more liberal and individualist societies, where the question of women's rights is so prominent. The burden of child care in large families tends to fall disproportionately on the mother, as with so many other aspects of the household economy. The emancipation of women, and the opportunity for many more to work full-time and to pursue careers, have meant both that the age at which couples have children has gradually increased, and that the number of children per family has tended to fall.

If the birth rate of a particular nation cannot be stimulated, the obvious solution is immigration.

Given the inequalities in the international economy, there are many citizens of poor countries willing to emigrate to work in rich countries. Such migrants are young, highly motivated, and prepared to work hard and for low wages. They pay taxes, and therefore make a major contribution to the resources available to the welfare state. Many additionally work directly for the welfare state, for example in hospitals and in social care. Contrary to tabloid myths, they tend to take very little out of the welfare state, unless they suffer an accident or illness, because many of them are working to earn money they send back to support their families in their home country. Immigration rejuvenates a nation's age profile, and if immigrants are allowed to settle and bring their families, then this, too, encourages a better demographic composition.

Immigration is the perfect solution for a country with an ageing population, but it has become one of the most toxic of political issues, with huge resistance from local communities to the impact that immigration is believed to have on housing, jobs, and schools. As so often before, migrants are made the scapegoat for shortcomings in other areas of policy, and myths quickly grow about the preferential treatment that migrants receive, and how their needs are given priority by the welfare state, ignoring the claims of other citizens. Some of the hostility to immigrants arises from the desire to defend the welfare state as an exclusive benefit for the national community. Some of it arises from fear of their competition for jobs and the impact on wages. The rise of anti-immigrant parties across Europe has changed the discourse about immigration, and more and more obstacles are being erected to stem the flow. But the problem seems unmanageable. Countries are not proving very effective in policing their borders or reducing the flow of migrants. They need them too much.

A policy of open borders will not fly politically, but equally a policy of closed borders would be unworkable, wrong, and counterproductive. As discussed earlier, some kind of managed immigration is the only way forward, and potentially it has an important part to play in relieving some of the pressures on the welfare state, particularly in relation to ageing populations. A market libertarian agenda would support open borders as a way of cutting costs and undermining support for collective welfare. If migrant workers do not expect welfare benefits, they can be deprived of them, which helps cuts employers' costs. They would not have to pay into pensions, for example. Indigenous workers then argue they are being undercut, but the market libertarian answer is that the way to stop being undercut is to give up the benefits too. In this way, the welfare state would start to unravel, fuelled by the social conflicts which high levels of immigration create.

The four challenges discussed in this chapter are all deep-rooted and together pose a number of intractable dilemmas for policy. Finding ways to manage them is essential to rekindle broad-based support for the principles of a universal welfare state. But what is also needed is a vision which can once again inspire hope and trust.

4

A Future for the Welfare State

Faced with all these challenges, can the welfare state survive? It has to change if it is to do so. That is nothing new. It has been changing throughout the last hundred years. Most of us could not imagine our societies without a welfare state. Few citizens would vote to dismantle it and give up their benefits. But its survival is not guaranteed. Like so many human constructions, if the political will and capacity to sustain it and adapt it disappear, the welfare state could wither away. The circumstances in which welfare states first arose and the circumstances in which they have to operate today are very different. An understandable response is to circle the wagons and defend the welfare state as it currently is. But that would make Paul Pierson's fears of its approaching demise come true. Yet the opposite extreme must also be guarded against. Too much change or the wrong kind of change can be damaging. Many things of value can be heedlessly lost. The welfare state, with its complex networks, institutions, and cultures, is a rich inheritance to be enjoyed and celebrated, not thrown away.

The Nordic social democracies have managed to adapt their welfare states incrementally and with a reasonable amount of consensus. In other welfare states there is less consensus, and change has often been abrupt, adversarial, and subject to repeated reversals, as one set of institutional structures succeeds another. Major restructurings are sometimes required, but they only really work when as wide a consensus as possible has been achieved. That is difficult in societies which are fundamentally divided and very unequal, and in which the idea of the welfare state is under constant attack. A downward spiral of declining trust and declining support can easily be initiated.

There is nothing irreversible about the welfare state. The state has never had a monopoly and it is not desirable that it should. Welfare can be provided in many different ways. If the welfare state does not survive, that does not mean that welfare will not survive. But it will become much more patchy, with many gaps, and there would have to be much more reliance upon the voluntary sector and once again upon households. Some wonder whether in rich, post-industrial societies that is becoming a better way to organize things. A fashionable rhetoric now proclaims a high-wage, low-tax, low-welfare society as the way to go. As John Hills has pointed out, one of the biggest problems confronting the welfare state is the lack of understanding we have of it, and the equation of welfare with means-tested income support for the poorest in society.[1] If the welfare state were to shrivel to this, the battle would be lost.

One of the main conditions for the survival of the welfare state is therefore a much wider understanding of the many different functions it performs. Far from undermining capitalism, welfare states have been an essential ingredient in capitalism's success. Every capitalist economy when it has reached a certain stage of development has acquired a welfare state, and today's rising powers are beginning to follow the same path. To counter over-saving in their population against the insecurities of the market economy, the Chinese are beginning to introduce a welfare safety net. Organizing welfare through the state serves many purposes – including legitimacy, nation-building, modernization, social peace, relief of poverty, social investment, pooling of risks, redistribution, and social justice. Welfare states appeal to social engineers as well as moralists.

But they were never designed to replace capitalism. As Stein Ringen has observed, welfare states have in general been an attempt to change the circumstances individuals and families live under without basically changing society.[2] Where they have succeeded, they have helped to reform capitalism in ways which have made it compatible with democracy. Welfare states depend upon the prosperity and continued profitability of the capitalist economy, while the capitalist economy has become dependent upon welfare states. There is a creative tension between them; each needs the other. Sometimes, as in the 1970s, and now again today, these tensions can grow, leading many on both right and left to argue that the relationship cannot work, and that sooner or later capitalism will want to be free of the burden it is carrying.

Welfare states have become such an integral part of mature capitalist democracies that it is reasonable to turn the question round and ask if capitalism can survive if welfare states are destroyed. Capitalism has often been viewed as a dynamic untamed economic system which constantly revolutionizes social and political arrangements, forcing change on societies and individuals whether they like it or not. It is both destructive and creative at the same time, but if the destructive side of capitalism becomes too dominant, everyone loses. Welfare states helped stabilize and correct some of the downsides of innovation and competition, and also increasingly have driven capitalism in new directions, for example by assisting the entry of women into the workforce, dramatically improving health and education, and creating demand for the goods and services the economy produces. Much conventional economic discourse still thinks of the public sector as unproductive and the private sector alone as the creator of wealth. But the role of the state is much more active than that. The interpenetration of states and markets means that neither can function without the other. Much public spending creates the conditions in which businesses can thrive. Capitalism is a dynamic economic system but only because there are institutions outside the capitalist market which perform functions which allow the conditions on which it depends to be reproduced.

The future prospects of the welfare state depend in part on whether welfare states can continue to perform these functions for capitalism, finding new ways to innovate that deepen human well-being, opening up new avenues for social investment and for social protection. The central aim of welfare states remains the abolition of poverty and dependency. Critics allege that established welfare states create dependency and have no interest in removing it. That danger exists if welfare states become too conservative and cease modernizing. Welfare states succeed the more they enable all citizens to become self-reliant and independent, but in order to accomplish that, welfare states have both to invest and to protect. Relying on only one of these strategies will not work. A modern welfare state has to overcome the perception that there is a sharp division between redistribution to help the poor, and investment in universal services for the majority.

How might this be done? There is no shortage of radical ideas for pushing forward the frontiers of the welfare state in the twenty-first century. Building the political support for them is much more difficult, just as building political support for dismantling the welfare state has proved challenging. In the new hard times, the temptation is simply to defend what already exists, but that will not be sufficient. If a new reform momentum cannot be established, welfare states risk succumbing to permanent deadlocks and inertia which may ultimately lead to their collapse.

One way to approach this question is to go back to the question posed at the beginning: at what point does the welfare state cease to be a welfare state? It is hard to imagine in the advanced capitalist democracies that the state would ever cease all involvement in providing welfare. But if the welfare state shrank so that all it was providing was a basic safety net of means-tested income support, that would no longer be a welfare state as it came to be understood in the course of the twentieth century. It would mean that state provision of welfare had become subordinate once more to the market, and in most areas the state would be replaced as a supplier of welfare by charities and families. For a welfare state to exist, a sphere beyond the market has to be created. Esping-Andersen's insight is correct: there has to be a sphere which supports the market but is not governed by it, a sphere which allows labour and human needs to be 'de-commodified', and acknowledges the priority of individuals' social rights over their market performance.[3]

The first requirement to revitalize this vision in today's world is to develop a strategy to achieve basic income, guaranteeing to every citizen a minimum level of support, regardless of contribution or need, which would not be means-tested. Such an income could either be given unconditionally or be dependent upon evidence of participation in socially useful activities, such as child care or voluntary work. There are supporters of both, but the underlying premise is the creation of a society in which no individual is forced to depend for their basic needs on an income derived from paid employment.[4] Determining that basic minimum is the crucial step. Above that minimum, individuals are free to earn more by participating in paid employment, but there is no compulsion to do so. The idea that individuals could be freed from the obligation to work meets deep cultural resistance, because of the fear that it would encourage idleness. But the counter-argument is that market economies will function much better if individuals have the security of knowing that at every stage of their lives they will receive basic protection. In households already asset-rich and income-rich, individuals work just as hard or even harder, but they have the time and space to take advantage of opportunities, make experiments. The safety net of a basic income helps to enlarge the range of their choices and their chances of finding work which engages them fully.

The way welfare states have developed can be seen as building towards the provision of a basic income. Negative income tax, tax credits, and minimum and living wages are all steps towards it. The cost is less than sometimes imagined, because many existing benefits would be rolled up in the basic income and those who also took paid jobs would pay tax on it. It would require a political culture which accepts the advantages of large transfers and therefore high taxation, but the Nordic welfare states have already demonstrated how that is compatible with an efficient and flourishing market economy. The gains in social cohesion, lower inequality, and high trust, overcoming many of the divisions which weaken the current welfare state and political support for it, make it an appealing arrangement. In societies where inequality has become much more entrenched, the welfare state is much more residual, and taxation is relatively low, the challenges for moving towards a basic income are much greater. But incremental change towards that objective is still possible, and the popularity of universal welfare schemes, once they are established, is indisputable, as the case of publicly funded health services and compulsory health insurance demonstrates. Building a political coalition around the idea of basic income would help end the resentment of those in work contributing to support those who are not able to work or cannot find jobs. Payment of a basic income to everyone would price workers into many more jobs which at present do not pay enough for people to live on.

A related idea is the proposal for capital grants, paid to every citizen on reaching a specified age, funded from an inheritance tax. In this way, a portion of capital would be recycled to every young adult, and would help to reduce the gross inequality in the ownership of assets, which are so important for life-chances. The same debate has existed over whether the use of grants should be conditional or unconditional and at what age they should be paid. But research has shown that the higher the amount of the initial grant, the greater the chance that it will be used wisely rather than recklessly.[5] If the grants were made conditional, they would have to be spent in a number of approved ways – such as house purchase, small business start-up, or training and further education. The purpose of such grants is an old idea which goes back to Tom Paine in the eighteenth century, that everyone should have the means to be independent and to pursue the life-course that is best for them.

Basic income and capital grants are both designed to make individuals more self-reliant and independent, to enlarge choice and aspiration, and to limit forms of dependency, which are stigmatizing and demoralizing. The active labour market policies of the Nordic welfare states take for granted that full employment is a necessary underpinning of a universal welfare state, but they take the stigma away from being unemployed. The advantage of a basic income is that while most individuals will choose to take jobs in the private or public sectors which give them higher earnings, careers, opportunities, and status, some individuals may choose to pursue occupations which are unpaid because of their intrinsic attraction or satisfaction. A few individuals may choose to be idle, but in a free society, that is a legitimate choice. Because everyone would receive basic income as a social right, a broad-based political consensus could be developed in support of these arrangements. The biggest obstacles holding back the development of the welfare state are the divisions and resentments between citizens over who is entitled to benefits, who is deserving and who is undeserving. Going back to the original impetus behind the welfare state – the creation of a democratic citizenship based on equal civil, political, and social rights – will help renew the political coalition for its preservation and extension.

Basic income and capital grants can only take us so far. Some of their advocates think that if the welfare state provides the means for every citizen to be self-reliant and independent, that ends the responsibility of the state. Some market libertarians are drawn to the idea of basic income as a way of reducing ever-increasing discretionary intervention by the state. But although reducing such discretionary intervention is an important goal, not everything can be left to individuals. Societies do not work like that, and trying to make them do so ends up increasing inequality and conflict. There are still important roles for social investment and social protection. Welfare states cannot be indifferent to the quality of health or education or social care services. Providing the opportunities through education and training so that all individuals can develop their skills and aptitudes and discover their abilities is an essential complement to a basic income strategy. Not all services have to be delivered by the state, but the state has an important role to ensure that the right quality and quantity of services are available and responsive to the needs of those who use them. Much of this reflects the positive agenda of the Third Way experiments in Europe with a social investment state, with its emphasis on life-long learning and investment in children, and much of the creative thinking which was developed at that time needs to be built on and extended.

Social investment needs to go hand in hand with social protection. Protecting individuals against old and new social risks requires not just helping citizens to look out for themselves, adapting to the circumstances and opportunities they encounter, but also, as Colin Crouch and Martin Keune have argued, actively shaping those circumstances and opportunities.[6] This is a conception of the welfare state which emphasizes the need to preserve its separateness from the market economy, to foster the creative tension between them so that the welfare state does not substitute itself for the market, but also does not become dependent on it. The task of the state is not just to equip individuals to deal with the risks they face, but also to seek to shape the circumstances which give rise to those risks. The best way to do this is to support institutions and rules which provide buffers, and limit some of the uncertainties which are at the core of modern experience. Individuals need to be free to make their own choices as much as possible, but to be enabled to do so, they need some collective protections against the uncertainties created by the way markets, financial institutions, and large corporations operate. Areas for state involvement include: active regulation of the labour market, ensuring individuals have employment rights and can join trade unions; regulation of the financial markets, to prevent the many abuses witnessed in the run-up to the 2008 crash and the destabilizing effects of uncontrolled financial flows; regulation of the housing markets, to provide protection against soaring housing costs; and regulation of companies, finding ways to improve corporate governance and involve a wider range of stakeholders in how companies are run, as well as ensuring support for different forms of ownership and different types of organization.

Any strategy for rebuilding the broad social consensus which the survival of the welfare state requires has to be launched in unpropitious political and economic circumstances. Rising inequality threatens to undermine social cohesion and reduce social mobility. If nothing is done, inequality may return to levels not seen since before the advent of the democratic era. The growing divide between rich and poor has been charted by Thomas Piketty, Tony Atkinson, and others.[7] Their datasets show how inequality reached a peak in the *Belle Époque* before the First World War. It then narrowed sharply as a result of the two world wars and the establishment of the extended welfare states of the post-war era. After the stagflation crisis of the 1970s, however, inequality began rising again. It was particularly marked in the Anglo-liberal welfare regimes, and more muted in the Nordic and corporatist welfare states. The welfare state is compatible with varying levels of inequality and it has never been part of its purpose to seek to eliminate inequality altogether. But it has been a central tenet of welfare regimes that one of the reasons for having a welfare state is to make life-chances more equal, to provide social minimums, and to create a common citizenship in which everyone enjoys civil, political, and social rights. The degree of inequality which is becoming common again in Western societies strikes at the compact which lies at the heart of the welfare state. As the rich have grown so much richer, they have become more detached from the societies in which they live, and many no longer contribute very much in terms of taxes, and do not use the services which are provided collectively for all citizens. They have their own hospitals, schools, shops, and gated communities.

Inequality poses another challenge to any renewal of the welfare state. This is the inequality between rich and poor countries. One manifestation of this is the rising tide of immigration. The number of economic migrants and asylum seekers trying to enter the rich countries has been sharply increasing. It has sparked sharp political reactions with the rise of populist anti-immigrant parties in many European countries, regardless of the type of welfare regime. These parties include the Swedish Democrats, the True Finns, the Party for Freedom in the Netherlands, the Front National in France, the UK Independence Party, the Northern League in Italy, and many more. Growing ethnic divisions in many of the rich democracies threaten the solidarity necessary to sustain an inclusive and universal welfare state. Ways are being sought to exclude immigrants from access to welfare state services and benefits which national citizens enjoy, and immigrants become a scapegoat for all the ills of the economy, particularly in times of recession.

The welfare state developed with nation-states, and the political consensus for it was constructed within national communities. It is hardly surprising that national governments are put under great pressure to defend their borders and the rights of their citizens, including the right to continue to enjoy high wages and a generous welfare state. The divisions which exist internationally put the divisions which exist within nation-states into perspective. The scale of the task can look hopeless. The European Union has made only small progress in arranging cross-national transfers within its borders. The task of organizing them across the whole world is still more daunting. But the world is changing and the need for common action to deal with common problems like climate change may help spur cooperation in other areas. The advantages to everyone in extending the protections which the rich countries enjoy are obvious, the means of doing so less so. A first step would be renewing the political consensus on the welfare state within nation-states. But if that leads to a defensive position to the rest of the world, it will be self-defeating. Only if it is treated as a step towards finding ways in which the best practices of the advanced welfare states can be extended to other countries, and a more equal world created, will national welfare states be secure in the long run.

Welfare states are part of the long project to extend citizenship rights to all. The struggle for basic fairness in areas like gender and generational equality is still far from over, but it now needs to be linked to the task of building a more sustainable economy in the face of rising inequality, austerity politics, and climate change. This requires the building of new coalitions and the development of new policies and new arguments. The moral case for trying to build more sustainable societies based on inclusive welfare arrangements which underpin strong cohesive democracies is a very strong one. The practical case for taking action to tackle all the ills which afflict us is also compelling. The obstacles are great, but so too is the prize.

Further Reading

A very good place to start is *The Welfare State Reader* edited by Christopher Pierson, Francis G. Castles, and Ingela K. Neumann (Cambridge: Polity, 2014). This combines classic readings from T.H. Marshall, Richard Titmuss, Claus Offe, and many more, with current debates and perspectives. Gøsta Esping-Andersen's *The Three Worlds of Welfare Capitalism* (Cambridge: Polity, 1990) is indispensable, as is Paul Pierson (ed.), *The New Politics of the Welfare State* (Oxford: Oxford University Press, 2001), and Chris Pierson, *Beyond the Welfare State: The New Political Economy of Welfare* (Cambridge: Polity, 1998). There are some excellent recent comparative studies of the welfare state which include Kees van Kersbergen and Barbara Vis, *Comparative Welfare State Policies* (Cambridge: Cambridge University Press, 2014), Colin Hay and Daniel Wincott, *The Political Economy of European Welfare Capitalism* (London: Palgrave-Macmillan, 2012), and Anton Hemerijck, *Changing Welfare States* (Oxford: Oxford University Press, 2013). For the politics of the welfare state, see the important studies by John Hills, *Good Times Bad Times: The Welfare Myth of Them and Us* (Bristol: Policy Press 2015), and Peter Taylor-Gooby, *The Double Crisis of the Welfare State and What We Can Do About It* (London: Palgrave-Macmillan, 2013). For feminist analyses of the welfare state, see in particular Carole Pateman, *The Disorder of Women* (Cambridge: Polity, 1989), and Ruth Pearson and Diane Elson, 'Transcending the impact of the financial crisis in the United Kingdom: towards plan F – a feminist economic strategy', *Feminist Review* 109 (2015), 8–30. For new social risks, see Guiliani Bonoli, 'The politics of the new social policies', *Policy and Politics* 33:3 (2005), 431–49. For basic income, the key text is Philippe van Parijs, *Real Freedom for All: What (If Anything) Can Justify Capitalism?* (Oxford: Oxford University Press, 1995), while the case for capital grants is eloquently put by Bruce Ackerman and Anne Alstott in *The Stakeholder Society* (New Haven, CT: Yale University Press, 2008). Inequality is well served at the moment with two major contributions from Thomas Piketty, *Capital in the Twenty-First Century* (Cambridge, MA: Harvard University Press, 2014), and Anthony B. Atkinson, *Inequality* (Cambridge, MA: Harvard University Press, 2015). Many of the issues we wrestle with now were dealt with elegantly and pointedly by James Meade over fifty years ago in *Efficiency, Equality and the Ownership of Property* (London: Allen & Unwin, 1964).

Notes

Introduction

1 John Hills, *Good Times, Bad Times: The Welfare Myth of Them and Us* (Bristol: Policy Press, 2015).

2 See Paul Pierson (ed.), *The New Politics of the Welfare State* (Oxford: Oxford University Press, 2001), and his later, post-crash assessment 'The welfare state over the very long run', ZeS Working Paper, 02/2011, http://econpapers.repec.org/paper/zbwzeswps/022011.htm.

3 Anton Hemerijck, *Changing Welfare States* (Oxford: Oxford University Press, 2013), p. 25.

4 Colin Hay and Daniel Wincott, *The Political Economy of European Welfare Capitalism* (London: Palgrave-Macmillan, 2012).

5 Vivien Schmidt and Mark Thatcher (eds), *Resilient Liberalism in Europe's Political Economy* (Cambridge: Cambridge University Press, 2013).

Chapter 1 The Life and Times of the Welfare State

1 Nicholas Timmins, *The Five Giants: A Biography of the Welfare State* (London: HarperCollins, 2001).

2 Seymour Martin Lipset, *Political Man* (London: Heinemann, 1960).

3 F.A. Hayek, *The Road to Serfdom* (London: Routledge, 1944).

4 Karl Polanyi, *The Great Transformation: The Political and Economic Origins of Our Time* (Boston: Beacon Books, 2001).

5 Roger Bacon and Walter Eltis, *Britain's Economic Problem: Too Few Producers* (London: Macmillan, 1976).

6 Robert Skidelsky, *Politicians and the Slump* (London: Macmillan, 1967).

7 Gøsta Esping-Andersen, *The Three Worlds of Welfare Capitalism* (Cambridge: Polity, 1990).

8 Paul Pierson, *Dismantling the Welfare State? Reagan, Thatcher and the Politics of Retrenchment* (Cambridge: Cambridge University Press, 1994).

9 Anthony Giddens, *The Third Way: The Renewal of Social Democracy* (Cambridge: Polity, 1998); Anthony Giddens, Patrick Diamond, and Roger Liddle (eds), *Global Europe: Social Europe* (Cambridge: Polity, 2006).

10 Claus Offe, 'Some contradictions of the modern welfare state', *Critical Social Policy* 2:2 (1982), 7–14.

11 Andrew Gamble, *Crisis without End? The Unravelling of Western Prosperity* (London: Palgrave-Macmillan, 2014).

12 Mark Blyth, *Austerity: The History of a Dangerous Idea* (Oxford: Oxford University Press, 2013).

Chapter 2 The Battle of Ideas

1 R.H. Tawney, *Equality* (London: Allen & Unwin, 1931).

2 Bo Rothstein, *Just Institutions Matter: The Moral and Political Logic of the Universal Welfare State* (Cambridge: Cambridge University Press, 1998).

3 Ruth Pearson and Diane Elson, 'Transcending the impact of the financial crisis in the United Kingdom: towards plan F – a feminist economic strategy', *Feminist Review* 109 (2015), 8–30; Carole Pateman, *The Disorder of Women* (Cambridge: Polity, 1989).

4 On the role of religion in shaping welfare states, see Philip Manow and Kees van Kersbergen, *Religion, Class Coalitions and Welfare States* (Cambridge: Cambridge University Press, 2009).

5 Robert Nozick, *Anarchy, State, and Utopia* (Oxford: Blackwell, 1974).

6 For an analysis of neo-liberal ideas, see Raymond Plant, *The Neo-Liberal State* (Oxford: Oxford University Press, 2010).

7 F.A. Hayek, *The Constitution of Liberty* (London: Routledge, 1960).

8 For an analysis of the Speenhamland system, see Fred Block and Margaret Somers, *The Power of Market Fundamentalism* (Cambridge, MA: Harvard University Press, 2014), chapter 5.

9 Hills, *Good Times, Bad Times*.

Chapter 3 Four Challenges

1 Paul Posner and Jon Blöndal, 'Democracies and deficits: prospects for fiscal responsibility in democratic nations', *Governance* 25:1 (2012), 11–34.

2 Larry Summers, 'US economic prospects: secular stagnation, hysteresis, and the zero lower bound', *Business Economics* 49 (2014), 65–73.

3 On the Laffer and Rahn curves, see Daniel J. Mitchell, 'Question of the week: what's the right point on the Laffer curve?', www.cato.org/blog/question-week-whats-right-point-laffer-curve.

4 Duane Swank, *Global Capital, Political Institutions, and Policy Change in Developed Welfare States* (Cambridge: Cambridge University Press, 2002); Dani Rodrik, *The Globalization Paradox: Why Global Markets, States and Democracy Can't Coexist* (Oxford: Oxford University Press, 2011).

5 See especially Peter Taylor-Gooby, *The Double Crisis of the Welfare State and What We Can Do About It* (London: Palgrave-Macmillan, 2013); Hills, *Good Times, Bad Times.*

6 Kees van Kersbergen and Barbara Vis, *Comparative Welfare State Policies* (Cambridge: Cambridge University Press, 2014).

7 Mike Power, *The Audit Society* (Oxford: Oxford University Press, 1997).

8 T.H. Marshall, *Citizenship and Social Class* (Cambridge: Cambridge University Press, 1950).

9 Richard Titmuss, *Commitment to Welfare* (London: Allen & Unwin, 1968).

10 Christopher Hood, David Heald, and Rozana Himaz (eds), *When the Party's Over: The Politics of Fiscal Squeeze in Perspective* (Oxford: Oxford University Press, 2014).

11 Andrew Geddes, *Immigration and the European Integration: Towards Fortress Europe* (Manchester: Manchester University Press, 2008).

12 Giuliani Bonoli, 'The politics of the new social policies', *Policy and Politics* 33:3 (2005), 431–49.

13 Milton Friedman, *Capitalism and Freedom* (Chicago: University of Chicago Press, 1962).

Chapter 4 A Future for the Welfare State

1 Hills, *Good Times, Bad Times*, p. 13.

2 Stein Ringen, *What Democracy Is For: On Freedom and Moral Government* (Princeton, NJ: Princeton University Press, 2007).

3 Esping-Andersen, *The Three Worlds of Welfare Capitalism*.

4 Philippe van Parijs, *Real Freedom for All: What (If Anything) Can Justify Capitalism?* (Oxford: Oxford University Press 1995); 'Basic income and the two dilemmas of the welfare state', *Political Quarterly* 67:1 (1996), 63–6.

5 Julian Le Grand and David Nissan, *A Capital Idea: Start-Up Grants for Young People* (London: Fabian Society, 2000); Rajiv Prabhakar, *The Assets Agenda: Principles and Policy* (London: Palgrave-Macmillan, 2008); Bruce Ackerman and Anne

Alstott, *The Stakeholder Society* (New Haven, CT: Yale University Press, 2008).

6 Colin Crouch and Martin Keune, 'The governance of economic uncertainty', in Giuliano Bonoli and David Natali (eds), *The Politics of the New Welfare State* (Oxford: Oxford University Press, 2012), 45–62.

7 Thomas Piketty, *Capital in the Twenty-First Century* (Cambridge, MA: Harvard University Press, 2014); Antony B. Atkinson, *Inequality* (Cambridge, MA: Harvard University Press, 2015).